Tactical Tal: Part I

Copyright © 2018 Lyudmil Tsvetkov

All rights reserved. No part of this publication may be reproduced, stored in a retrieval system or transmitted in any form or by any means, electronic, electrostatic, magnetic tape, photocopying, recording or otherwise, without prior permission of the author.

Table of Contents

Introduction

This book presents the exceptional tactics of Mikhail Tal. The first part includes puzzles from his game collection from the period 1949-1960, just before he became world champion.

The puzzles are split in 3 sections, comprising beginner, intermediate and advanced tactics. Puzzles 1-142 feature beginner tactics, 143-245 intermediate ones and the rest advanced tactics.

All positions have been thoroughly checked with Stockfish chess engine, to remove any possible inconsistencies.

Tal tactics are a very special category of tactics, there are few similar tactical collections. Above Tal, there is only Stockfish who understands tactics better. Tal played a peculiar chess, based almost exclusively on piece interaction, and that is reflected in the puzzles featured.

I felt great joy browsing and analysing this game/puzzle collection. Each and every example is highly unusual, bizarre and surprising, something you will not see with any other human tactics puzzle collection. That fact inevitably rivets your attention.

What you will learn after studying this book:
- the great moves Tal made during this period
- how to handle unusual tactical situations
- the correct assessment of many positions
- where Tal went wrong

And, of course, I have no doubt at all you will get an enormous satisfaction from studying the examples. Tal is simply like that. Even if you don't feel great, Tal will make you so.

One peculiarity about the book is that it includes also quiet tactical moves, something most other books on tactics lack. The approach is also much more practical, including real game situations and not just some positions with a single winning line. That is why, where necessary, all relevant subvariations are explained in detail.

I have analysed to a bigger depth all more complicated positions, so you might be more or less certain the positional assessment given is the correct one. That is one more issue with some manuals.

Finally, some words of persuasion - get this book, study it carefully, and you can not but be happy. The beneficial effect of getting in touch with a tactical genius is such, that, even if you don't learn everything, you are bound to be grateful for the exceptional quality and uniqueness of the chess featured.

April 2018

The Puzzles

Beginner Tal

1) White to play

2) Black to play

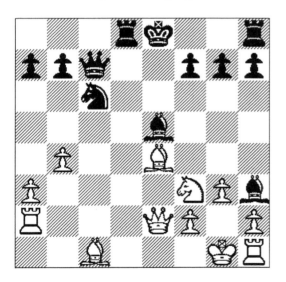

4) White to play

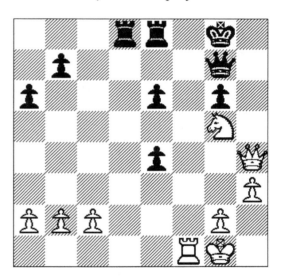

5) White to play

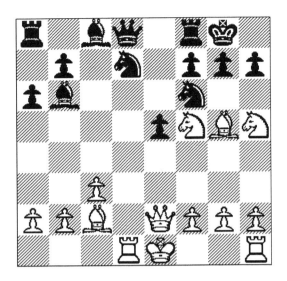

7) Black to play

6) White to play

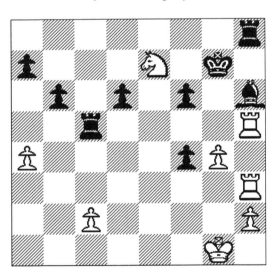

8) Black to play

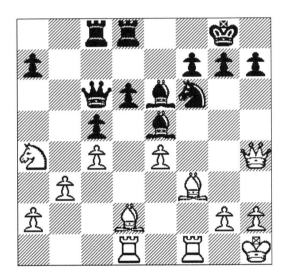

9) Black to play

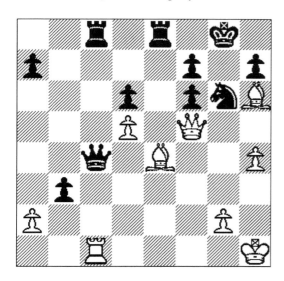

11) White to play

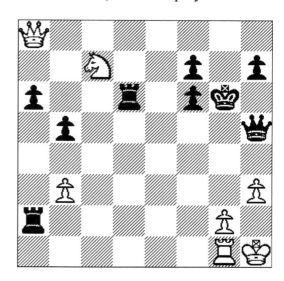

10) White to play

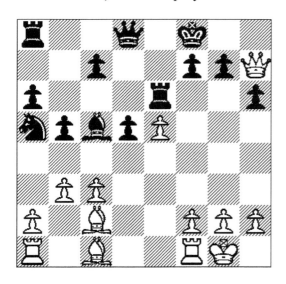

12) Black to play

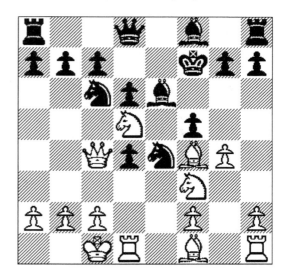

13) White to play

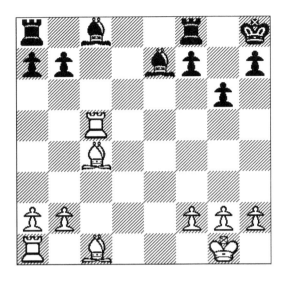

15) Black to play

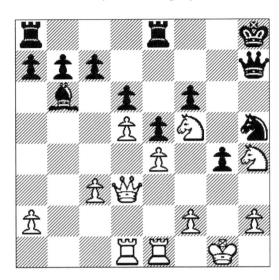

14) White to play

16) Black to play

17) White to play

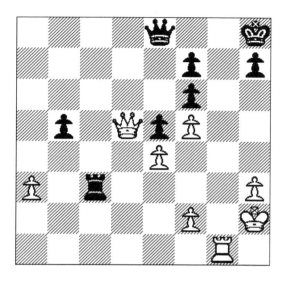

19) White to play

18) White to play

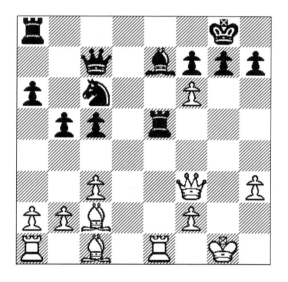

20) Black to play

21) White to play

23) White to play

22) White to play

24) Black to play

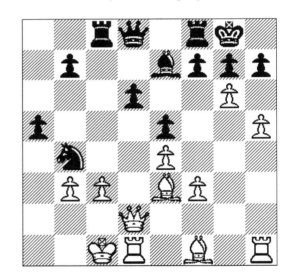

8

25) White to play

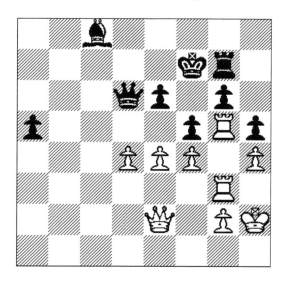

26) White to play

27) White to play

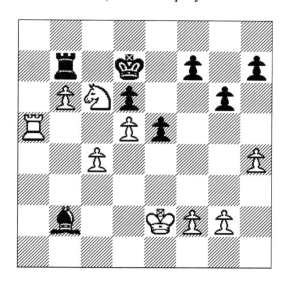

28) Black to play

29) White to play

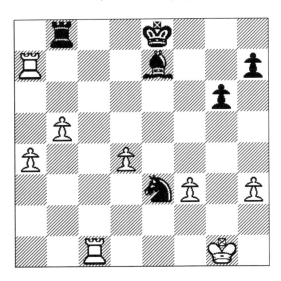

31) White to play

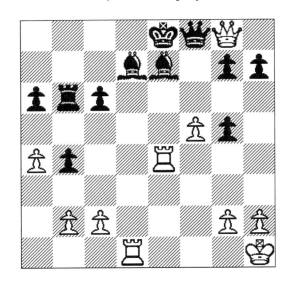

30) White to play

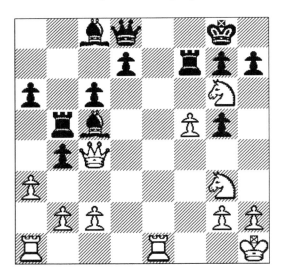

32) White to play

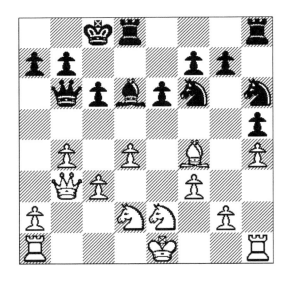

10

33) Black to play

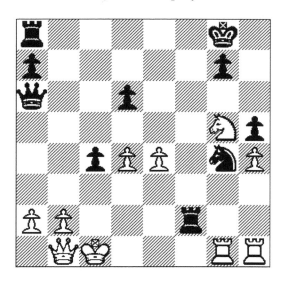

35) White to play

34) Black to play

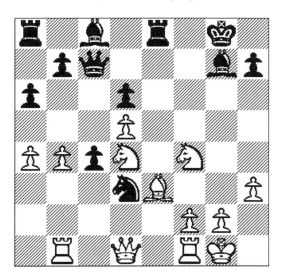

36) White to play

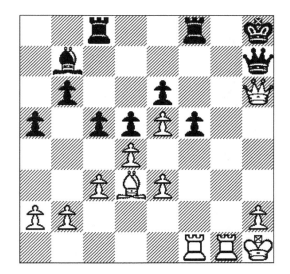

37) White to play

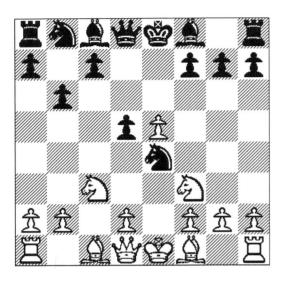

39) Black to play

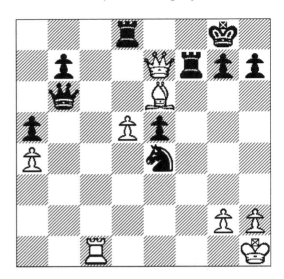

38) White to play

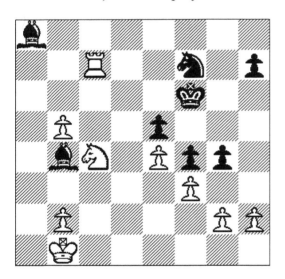

40) Black to play

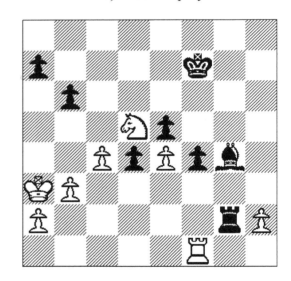

41) White to play

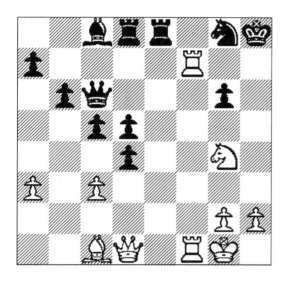

42) White to play

43) Black to play

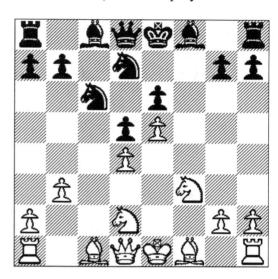

44) Black to play

13

45) White to play

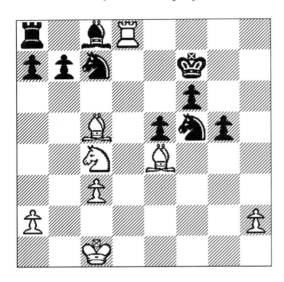

47) Black to play

46) Black to play

48) White to play

49) White to play

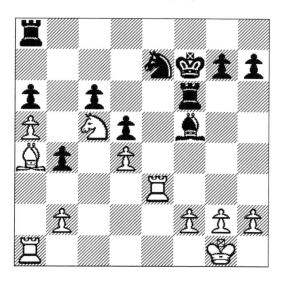

51) Black to play

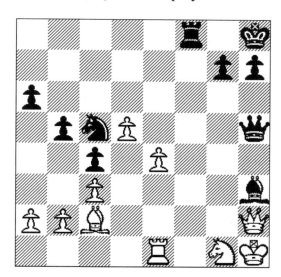

50) White to play

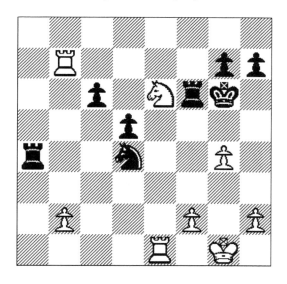

52) Black to play

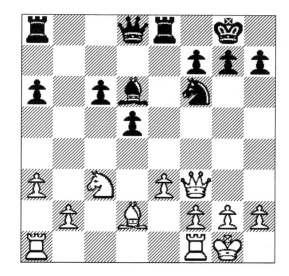

53) Black to play

55) White to play

54) Black to play

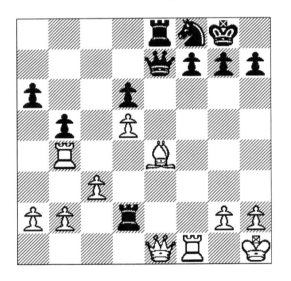

56) Black to play

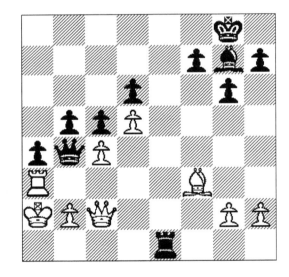

57) White to play

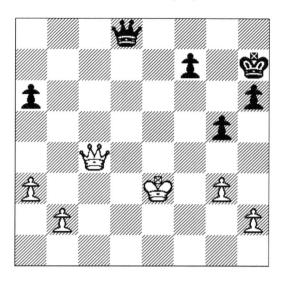

59) Black to play

58) White to play

60) Black to play

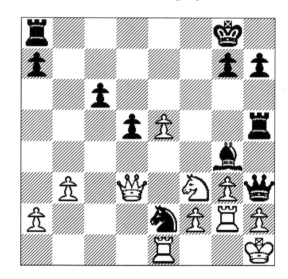

61) White to play

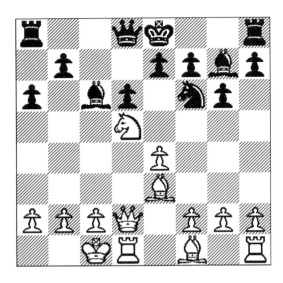

63) White to play

62) White to play

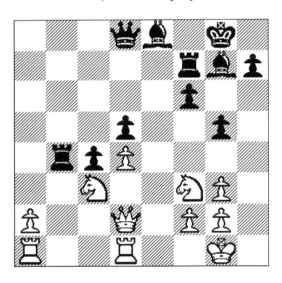

64) Black to play

18

65) White to play

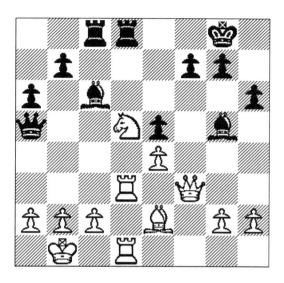

67) Black to play

66) White to play

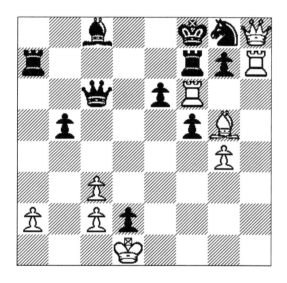

68) Black to play

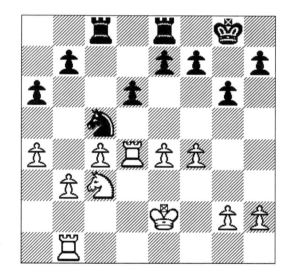

69) Black to play

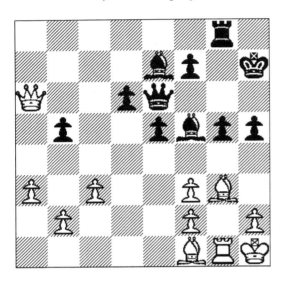

71) Black to play

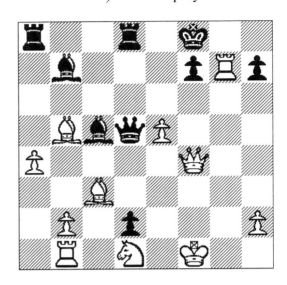

70) White to play

72) White to play

73) Black to play

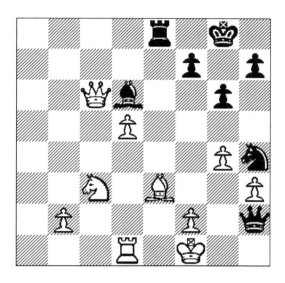

75) Black to play

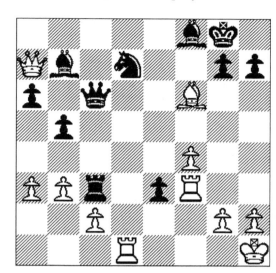

74) White to play

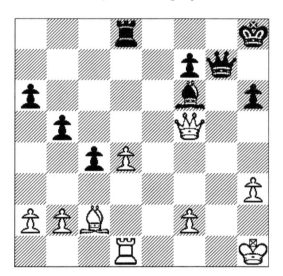

76) White to play

21

77) White to play

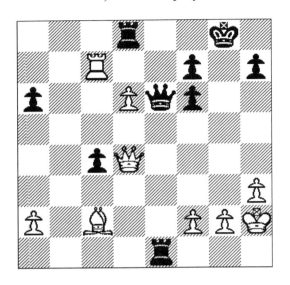

79) White to play

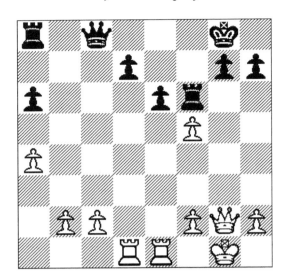

78) White to play

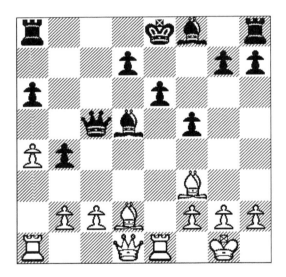

80) Black to play

81) Black to play

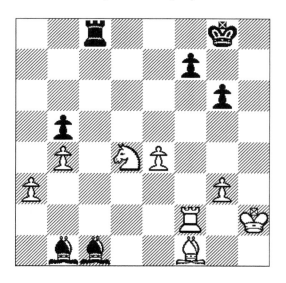

82) Black to play

83) Black to play

84) White to play

85) White to play

87) White to play

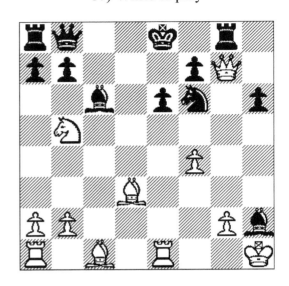

86) White to play

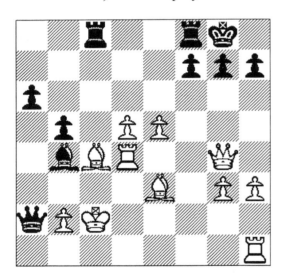

88) White to play

89) Black to play

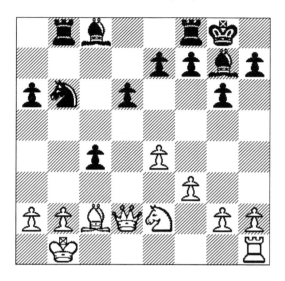

90) Black to play

91) Black to play

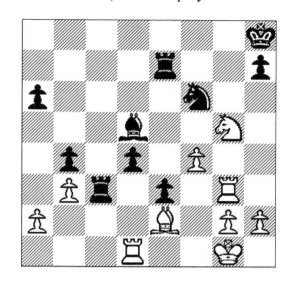

92) Black to play

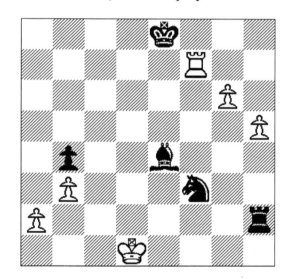

93) Black to play

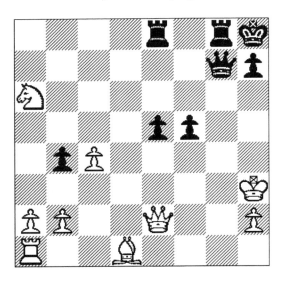

95) White to play

94) White to play

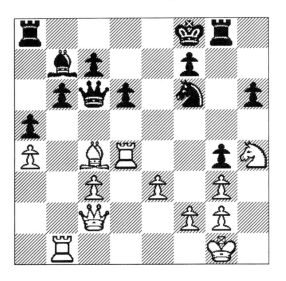

96) Black to play

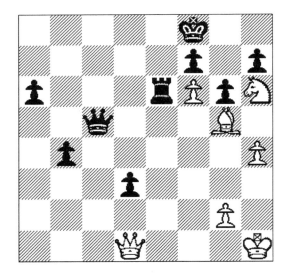

97) White to play

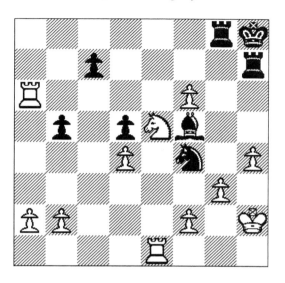

99) White to play

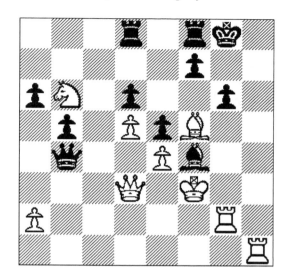

98) White to play

100) White to play

101) Black to play

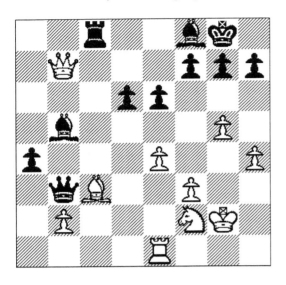

103) Black to play

102) Black to play

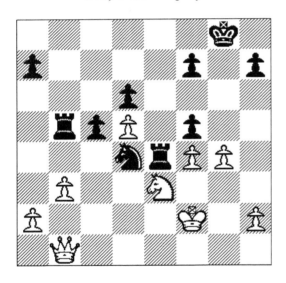

104) White to play

28

105) White to play

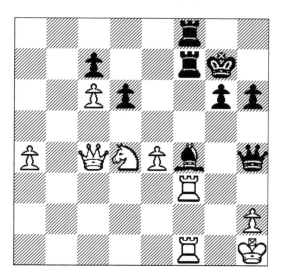

107) Black to play

106) Black to play

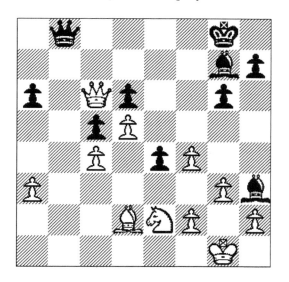

108) White to play

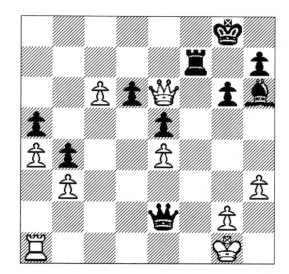

29

109) White to play

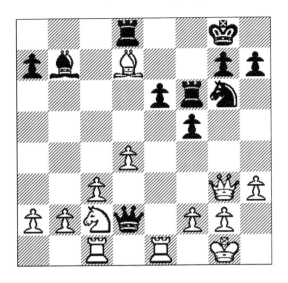

111) White to play

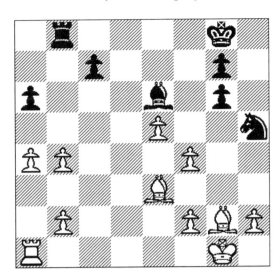

110) White to play

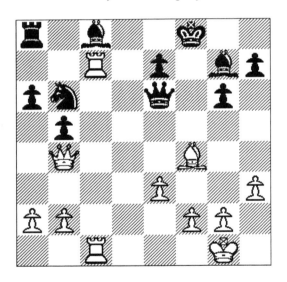

112) Black to play

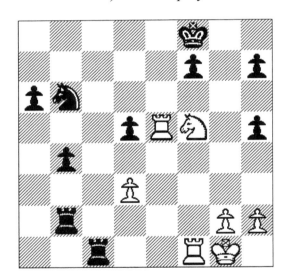

113) Black to play

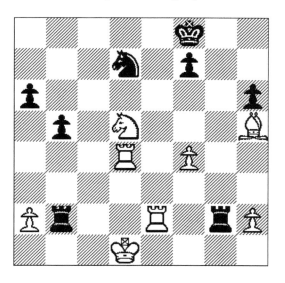

115) White to play

114) Black to play

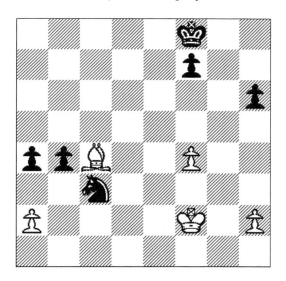

116) White to play

117) White to play

119) Black to play

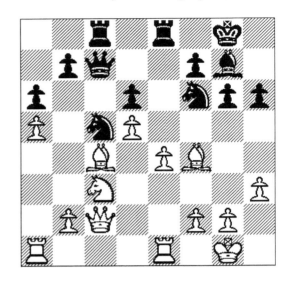

118) White to play

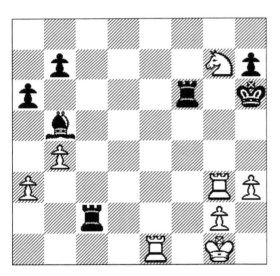

120) White to play

121) White to play

123) White to play

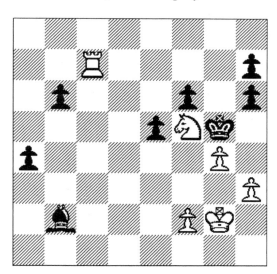

122) White to play

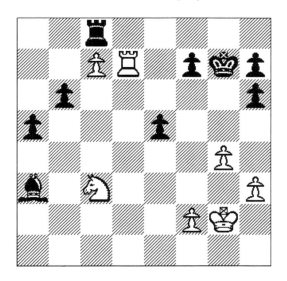

124) White to play

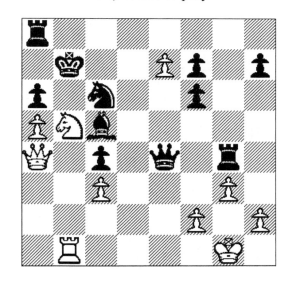

125) White to play

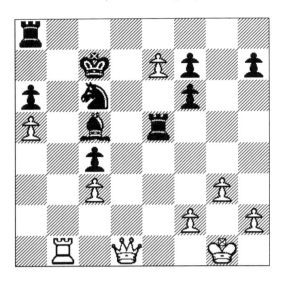

127) White to play

126) Black to play

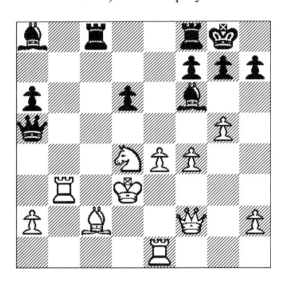

128) Black to play

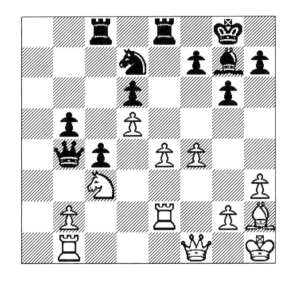

34

129) White to play

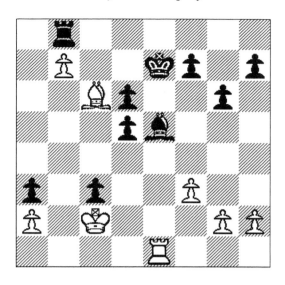

131) Black to play

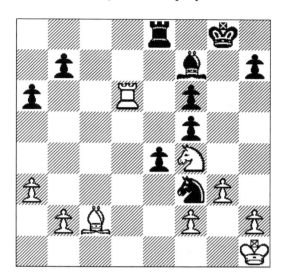

130) White to play

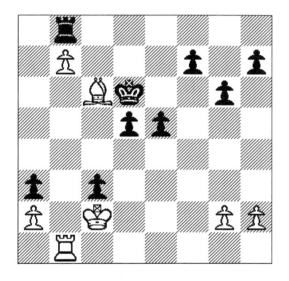

132) Black to play

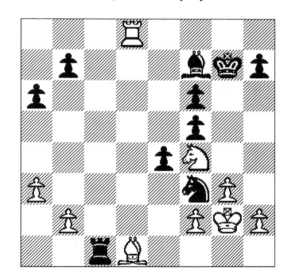

35

133) White to play

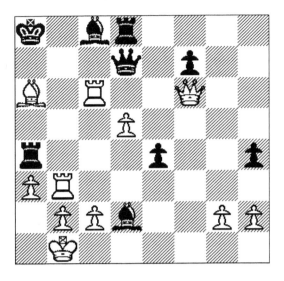

135) White to play

134) White to play

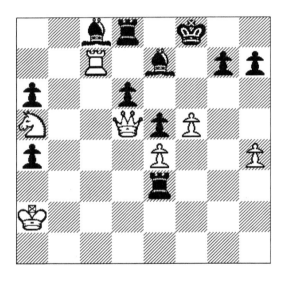

136) Black to play

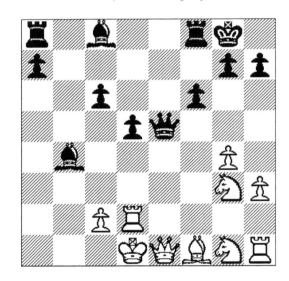

36

137) White to play

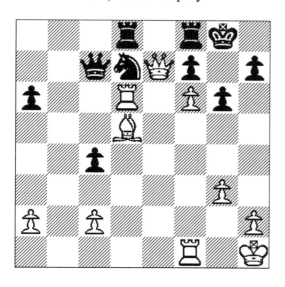

139) White to play

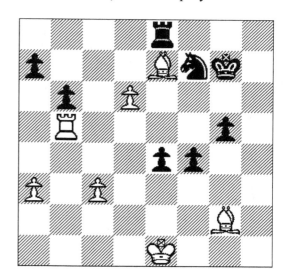

138) Black to play

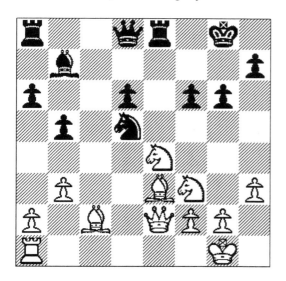

140) White to play

141) Black to play

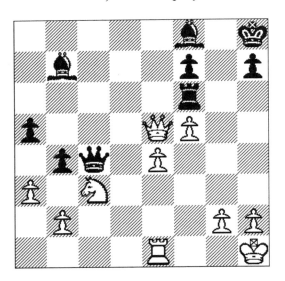

142) White to play

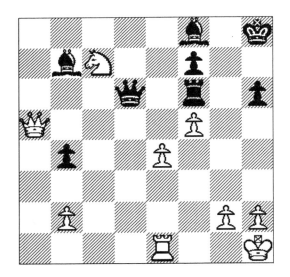

143) White to play

144) Black to play

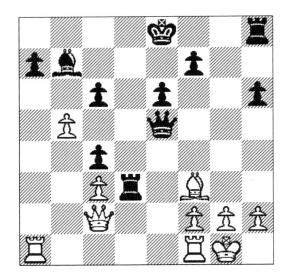

145) Black to play

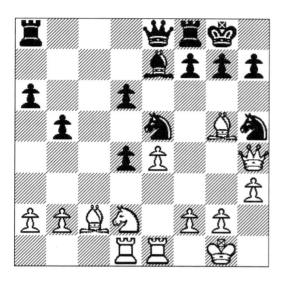

147) Black to play

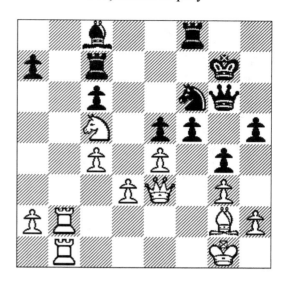

146) White to play

148) Black to play

39

149) Black to play

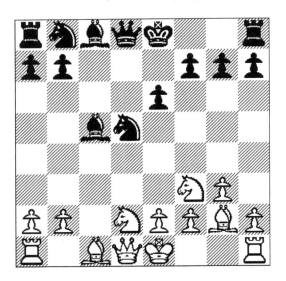

151) Black to play

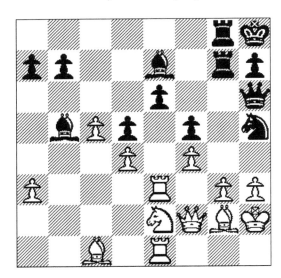

150) Black to play

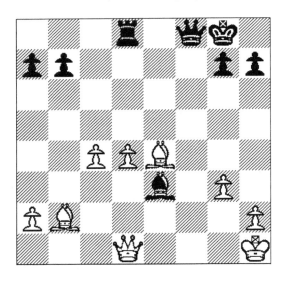

152) Black to play

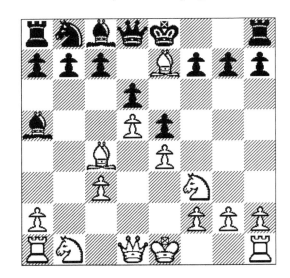

153) White to play

155) White to play

154) White to play

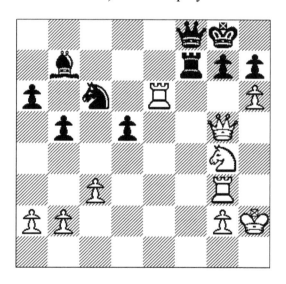

156) White to play

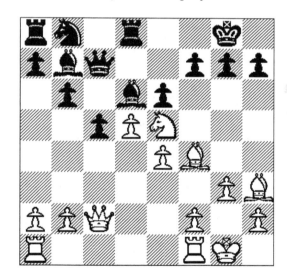

157) White to play

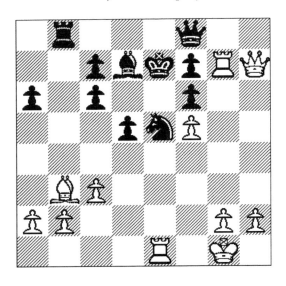

159) White to play

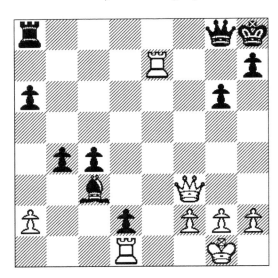

158) White to play

160) White to play

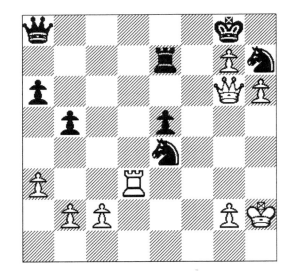

161) White to play

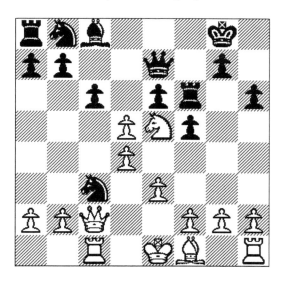

163) Black to play

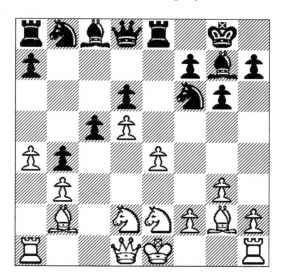

162) Black to play

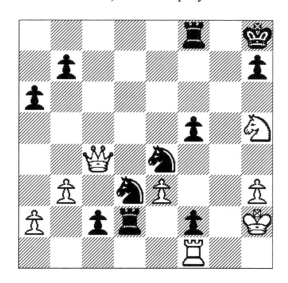

164) Black to play

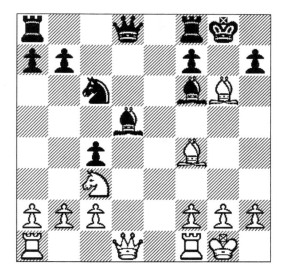

165) Black to play

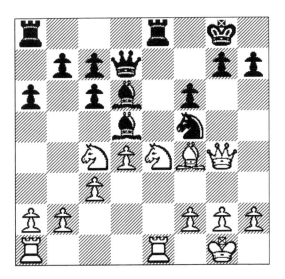

167) White to play

166) White to play

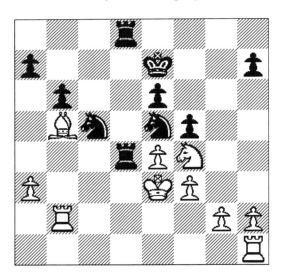

168) Black to play

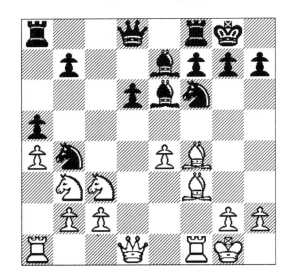

169) White to play

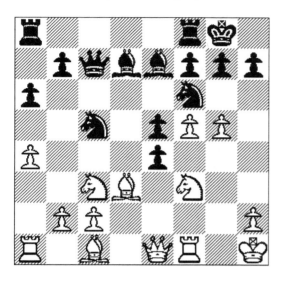

171) Black to play

170) Black to play

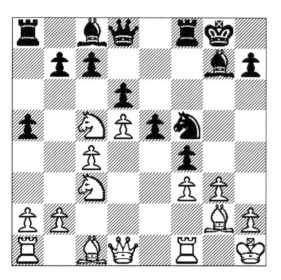

172) White to play

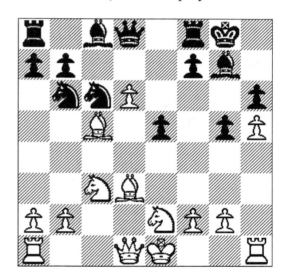

173) Black to play

175) White to play

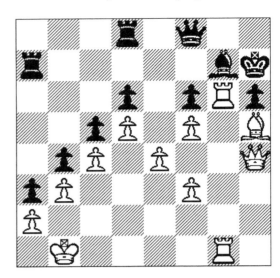

174) Black to play

176) White to play

177) White to play

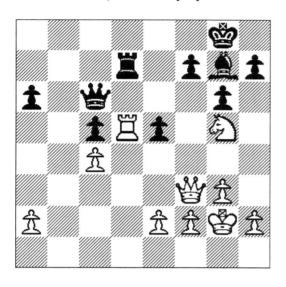

179) Black to play

178) Black to play

180) White to play

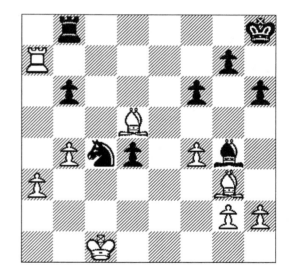

181) Black to play

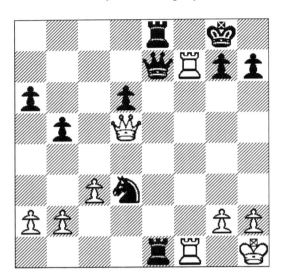

183) White to play

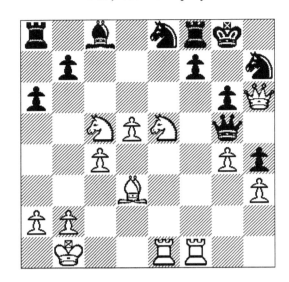

182) Black to play

184) Black to play

48

185) Black to play

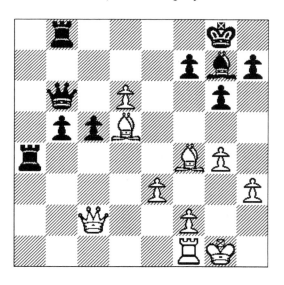

187) White to play

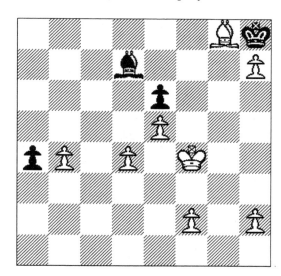

186) White to play

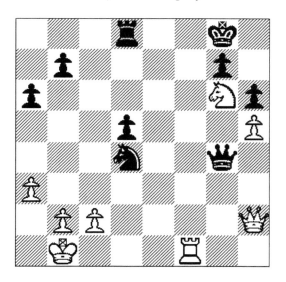

188) White to play

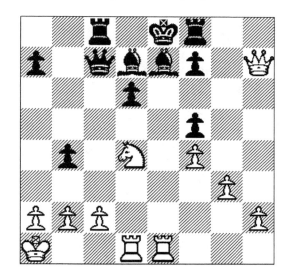

189) Black to play

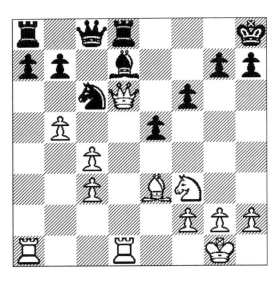

191) Black to play

190) Black to play

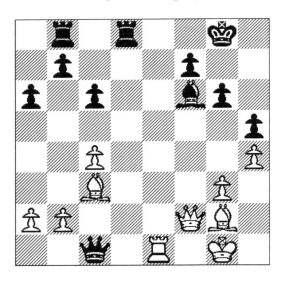

192) Black to play

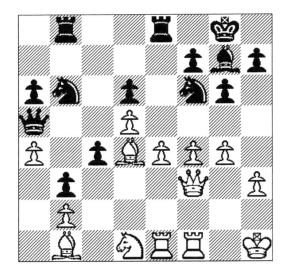

193) Black to play

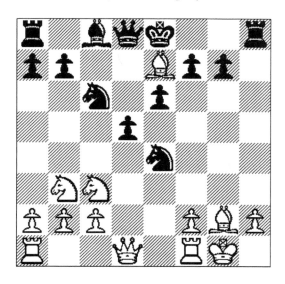

195) Black to play

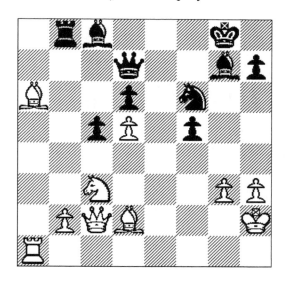

194) White to play

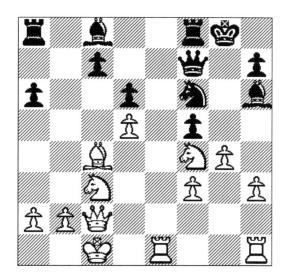

196) White to play

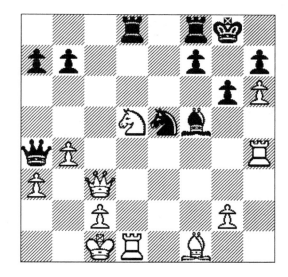

51

197) Black to play

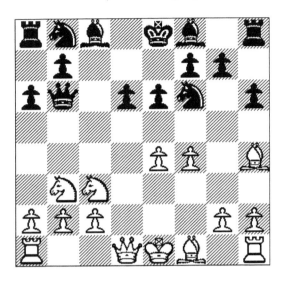

199) White to play

198) Black to play

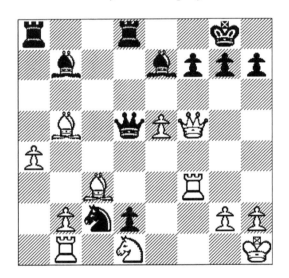

200) White to play

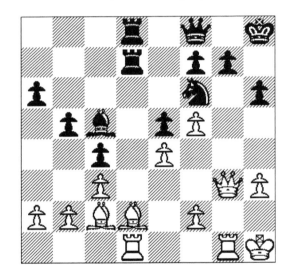

201) White to play

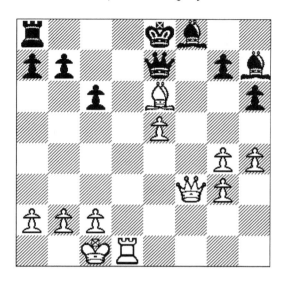

203) Black to play

202) White to play

204) Black to play

205) Black to play

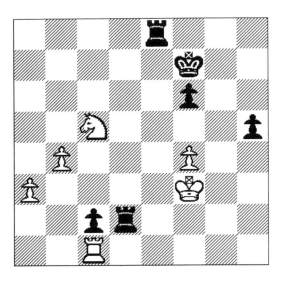

207) White to play

206) White to play

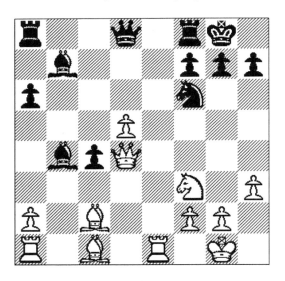

208) Black to play

209) Black to play

211) Black to play

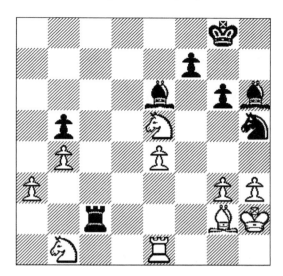

210) Black to play

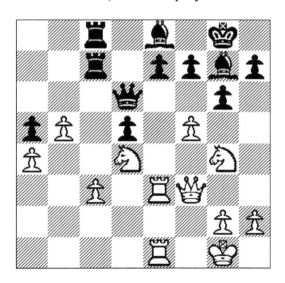

212) White to play

213) White to play

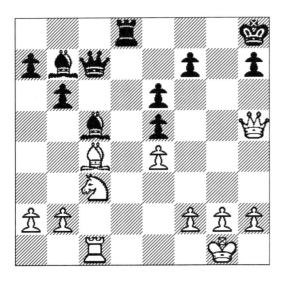

215) White to play

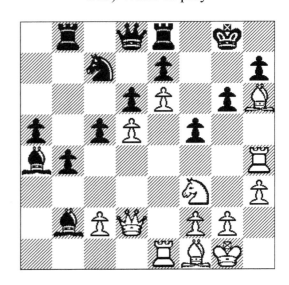

214) White to play

216) Black to play

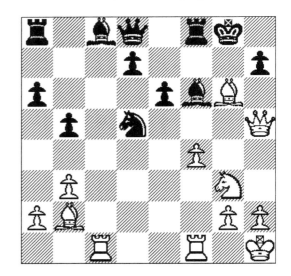

56

217) Black to play

219) White to play

218) White to play

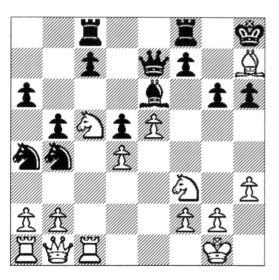

220) White to play

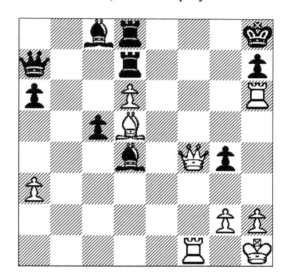

221) White to play

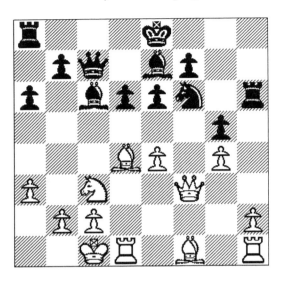

222) White to play

223) Black to play

224) Black to play

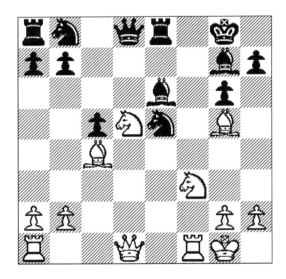

225) White to play

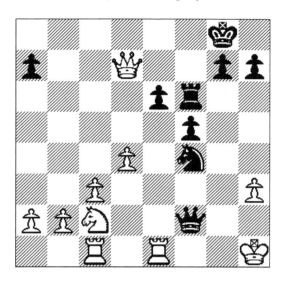

227) White to play

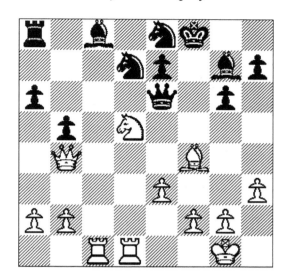

226) White to play

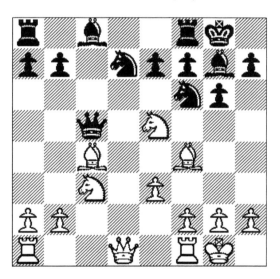

228) White to play

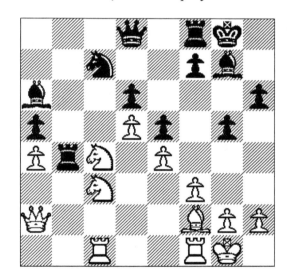

229) White to play

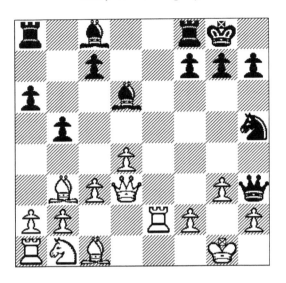

231) White to play

230) Black to play

232) White to play

233) Black to play

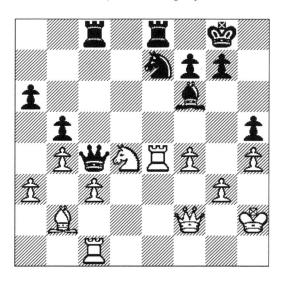

235) Black to play

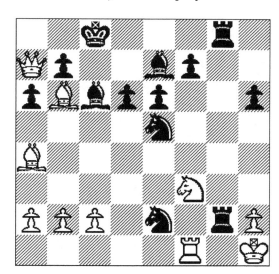

234) White to play

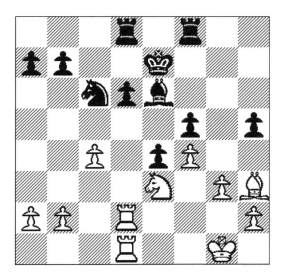

236) Black to play

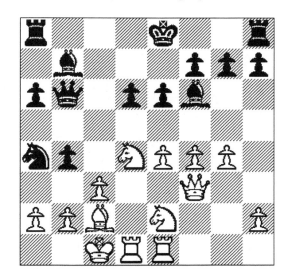

61

237) Black to play

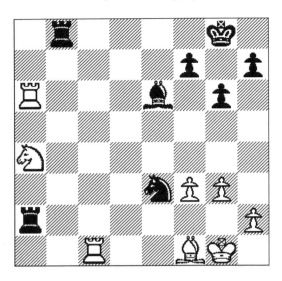

239) Black to play

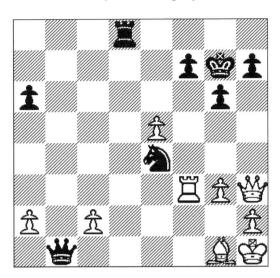

238) White to play

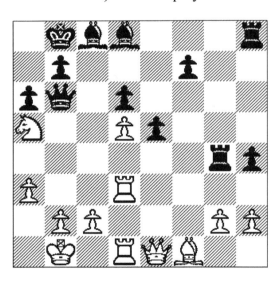

240) White to play

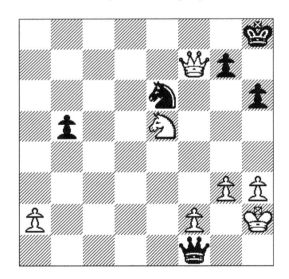

241) Black to play

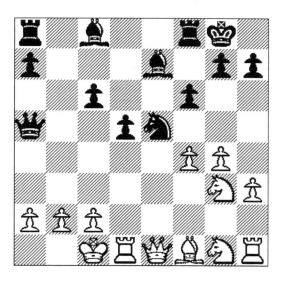

243) White to play

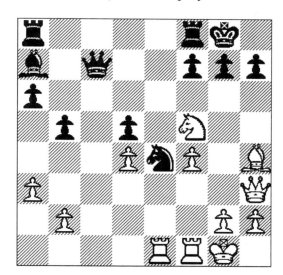

242) Black to play

244) White to play

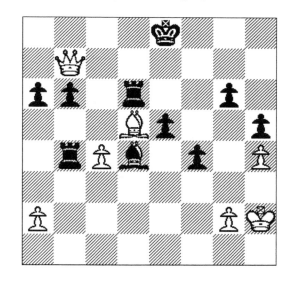

245) White to play

247) Black to play

248) Black to play

Advanced Tal

246) White to play

249) Black to play

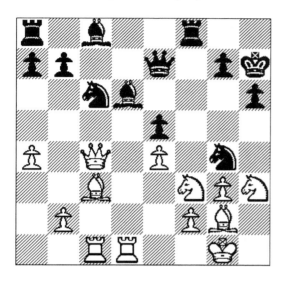

251) Black to play

250) Black to play

252) White to play

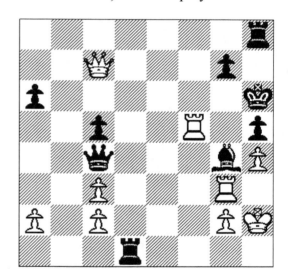

253) Black to play

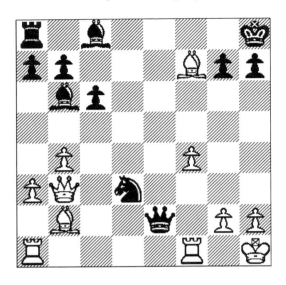

255) White to play

254) Black to play

256) Black to play

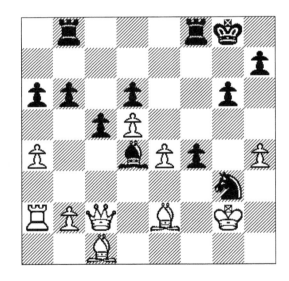

257) Black to play

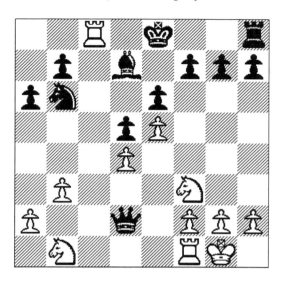

259) Black to play

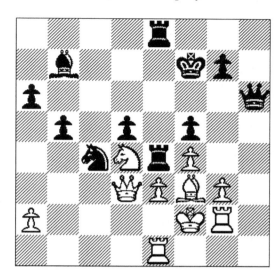

258) Black to play

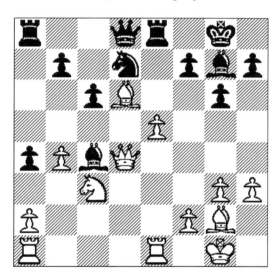

260) White to play

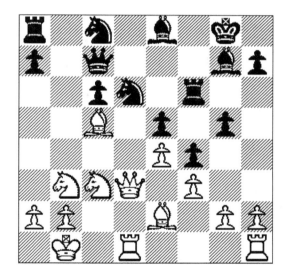

261) Black to play

263) Black to play

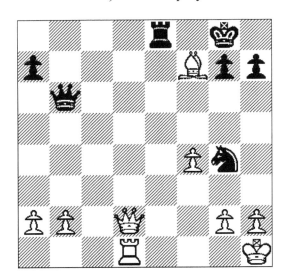

262) White to play

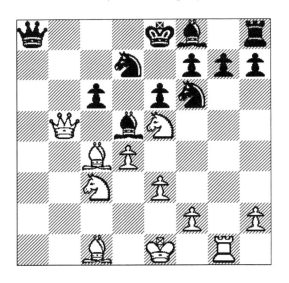

264) Black to play

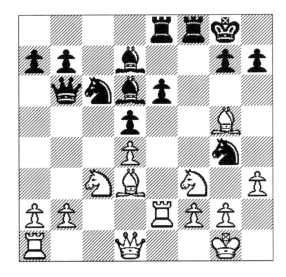

265) White to play

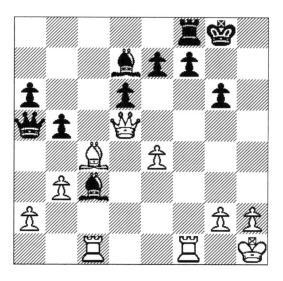

267) White to play

266) White to play

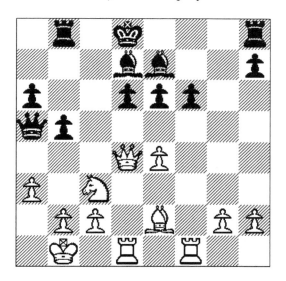

268) White to play

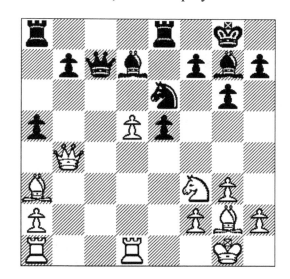

269) Black to play

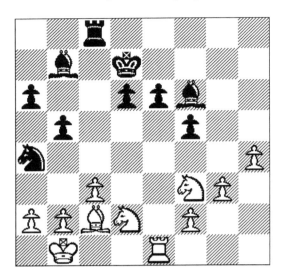

271) White to play

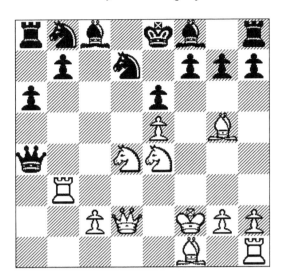

270) White to play

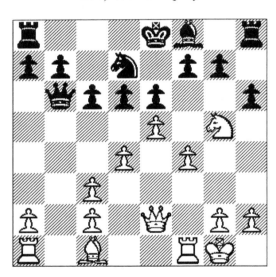

272) White to play

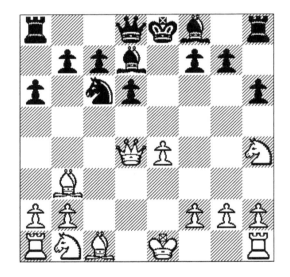

70

273) White to play

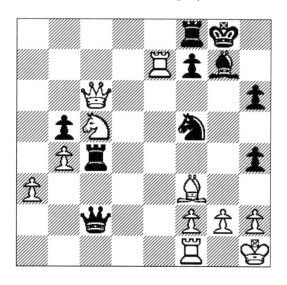

275) White to play

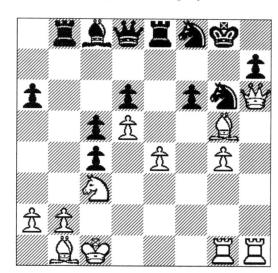

274) Black to play

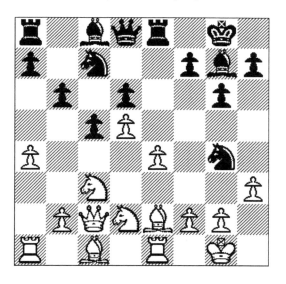

276) Black to play

277) White to play

279) White to play

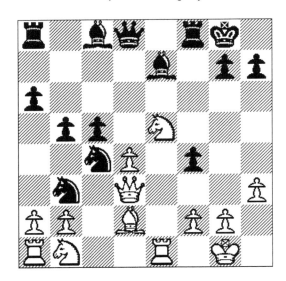

278) Black to play

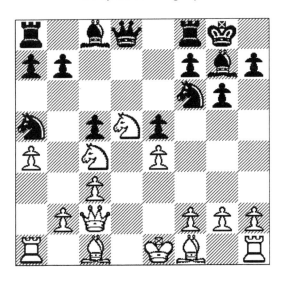

280) White to play

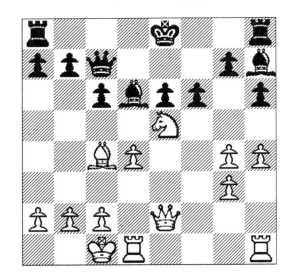

281) White to play

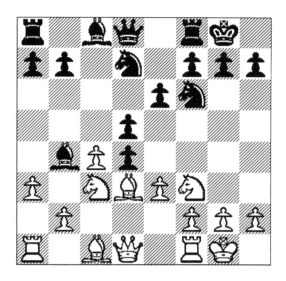

283) Black to play

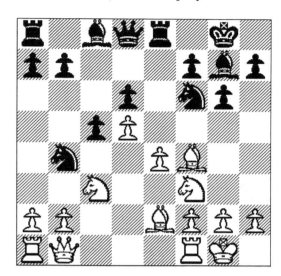

282) White to play

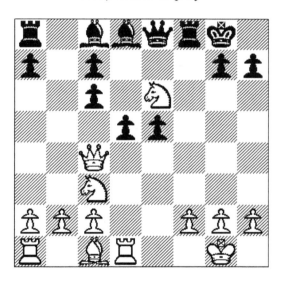

284) White to play

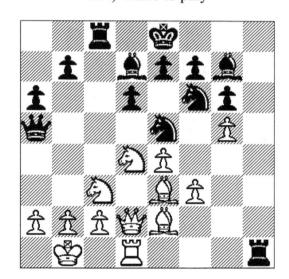

285) Black to play

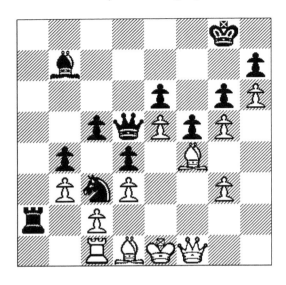

287) Black to play

286) Black to play

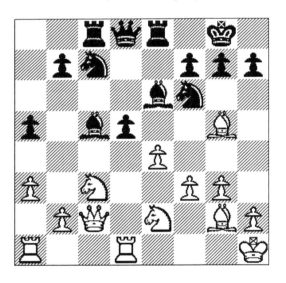

288) White to play

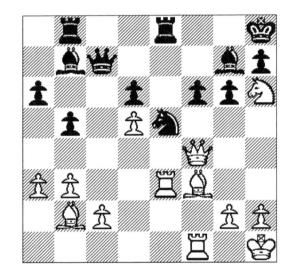

74

289) Black to play

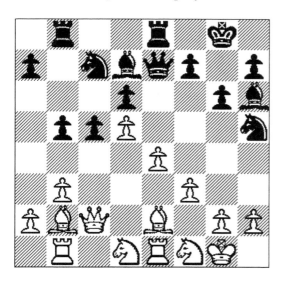

291) White to play

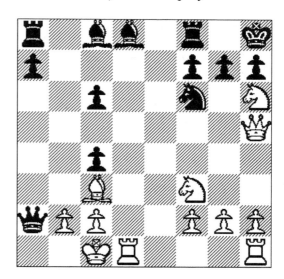

290) Black to play

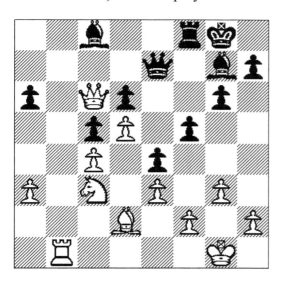

292) White to play

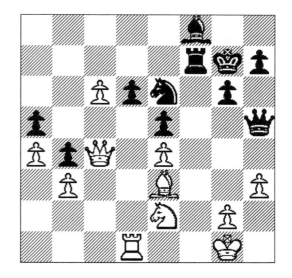

293) White to play

295) Black to play

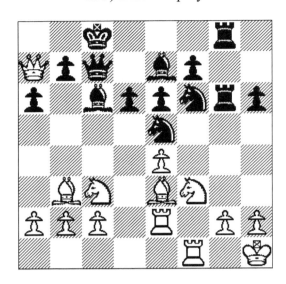

294) Black to play

296) White to play

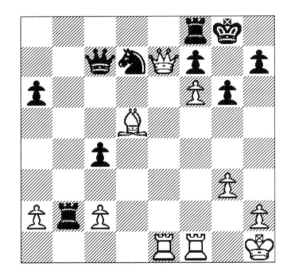

297) White to play

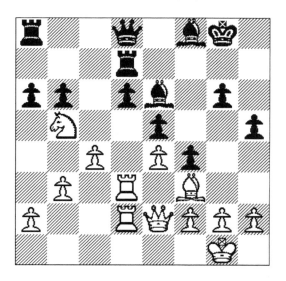

299) White to play

298) White to play

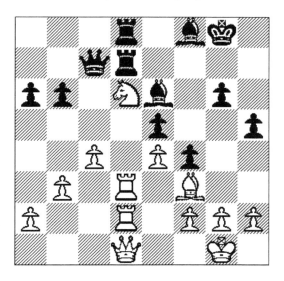

300) White to play

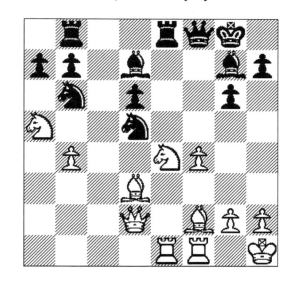

The Solutions

Beginner Tal

1) White to play

24. Nd4! 1-0 24...Rxe5 25. Nxc6 and white later wins the trapped bishop on h5.

Tal-Knaak, Halle 1949

2) Black to play

17...Nd4! easily converts the large positional advantage:
a) 18. Nxd4 Qxc1+ is a back rank mate
b) 18. Qe1 f5! 19. Nd4 fxe4 leaves black fully winning

Klovans-Tal, Riga 1949

3) White to play

25. Qe5+ forks the king and rook on c7

Tal-Leonov, Riga 1949

4) White to play

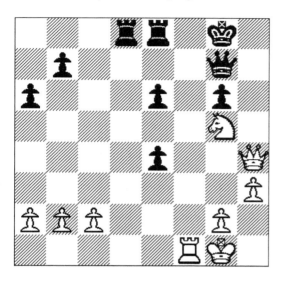

31. Nxe6 gets the exchange back, forking queen and rook(Rxe6 Qxd8+).

Tal-Ripatti, Riga 1949

5) White to play

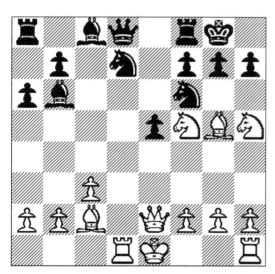

16. Bxf6! wins:
a) 16...Nxf6 17. Rxd8 picks up the queen
b) 16...gxf6 17. Qg4+, followed by mate on g7

Tal-Strelkov, Riga 1949

6) White to play

35. Nf5+ Kg6 36. Rxh6+ Rxh6 37. Rxh6+ leaves white in a winning position.

Tal-Kliavin, Latvia 1950

7) Black to play

35...Qf3+ 36. Qxf3 exf3 and then supporting the f3-pawn with the g-pawn after g5-g4 creates 2 connected passed pawns that will win the game.

Klasup-Tal, Riga 1950

8) Black to play

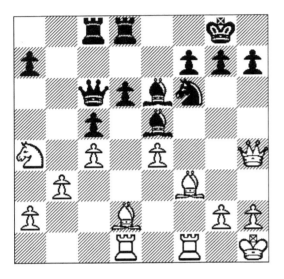

23...Bxc4! wins a pawn. Recapturing on c4 with the pawn is weak, as after 24. bxc4 Qxa4 the a2 and c4-pawns become isolated.

Lavrinenko-Tal, Riga 1950

9) Black to play

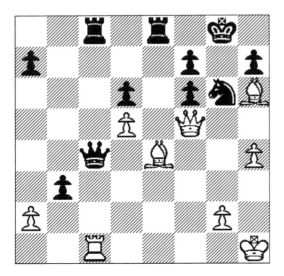

36...Qxc1+! 37. Bxc1 Rxc1+ 38. Kh2 bxa2, followed by promoting the a-pawn, seals the game.

Lavrinenko-Tal, Riga 1950

10) White to play

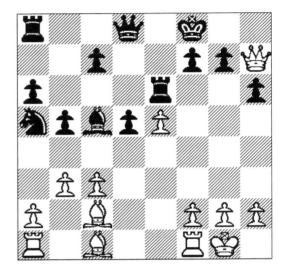

19. b4 forks knight and bishop.

Tal-Miglan, Riga 1950

11) White to play

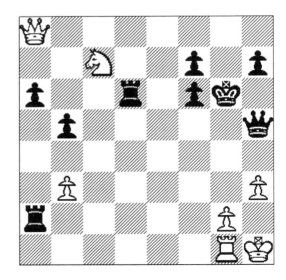

36. Qg8+ Kf5 37. g4+ is a royal fork.

Tal-Pliss, Riga 1950

12) Black to play

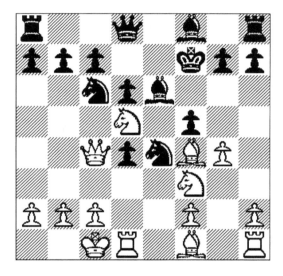

10...Ne7! adds another attacker to the pinned knight on d5, winning material.

Gutnikov-Tal, Leningrad 1951

13) White to play

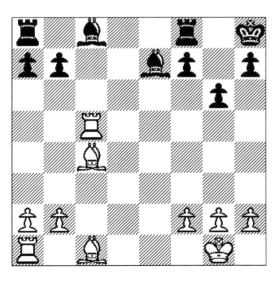

18. Rc7!, and after the retreat of the e7-bishop white takes the f7-pawn.

Tal-Giterman, Leningrad 1951

14) White to play

63. Bb5 is the end of it:
a) 63...Bf7 64. Bxa4 picks up another pawn
b) trading bishops transposes into a winning pawn endgame

Tal-Giterman, Leningrad 1951

15) Black to play

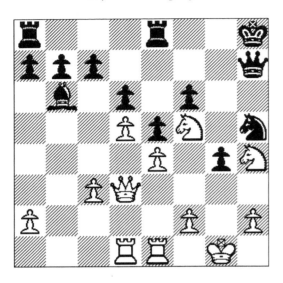

29...Nf4!, a tempo-gaining knight attack, later black will play Nh3+ and take on f2.

Klovans-Tal, Riga 1951

16) Black to play

40...Qc8+ forks king and rook.

Ragozin-Tal, Riga 1951

17) White to play

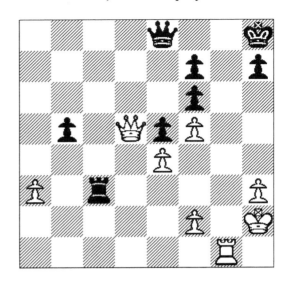

39. Qd2!, attacking the rook on c3 and, after the rook retreats somewhere or the black queen defends it, 40. Qh6 will follow, threatening simultaneously the g7 and f6 squares, from which there is no defence.

Tal-Fride, Riga 1951

18) White to play

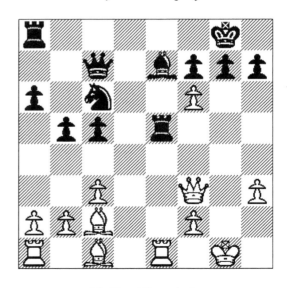

23. Rxe5! seals it:

a) 23...Ne5 24. Qxa8+
b) 23...Qxe5 24. Qxc6
23. fxe7?? Rxe1+ loses.

Tal-Gradus, Riga 1951

19) White to play

18. f5 Bxf5 19. Nxf5 Bxe3 20. Nxe3
Rfe8 21. Kf2 wins white a piece.

Tal-Zeid, Riga 1951

20) Black to play

44...Nh3+ 45. Kh1 Nxg5+ 46. Kg1
Bh2+ mates(47. Kh1 Bg3+ 48. Kg1
Nh3+ 49. Kh1 Nxf2++ 50. Kg1 Rh1#).

Blek-Tal, Latvia 1952

21) White to play

20. Ne6+ is a royal fork.

Tal-Darznieks, Riga 1952

22) White to play

33. Rd7+ and then 34. Rxa7 picks up the important a7-pawn, creating white a-passer, easily winning the game.

Tal-Skuja, Latvia 1952

23) White to play

29. Rxd7 Rxd7 30. Ne6+ is a royal fork.

Tal-Segal, Riga 1952

24) Black to play

18...Rxc3+ seals it:
a) 19. Qxc3 Na2+
b) 19. Kb1 Rb3+
c) 19. Kb2 Rc2+

Aevski-Tal, Soviet Union 1952

25) White to play

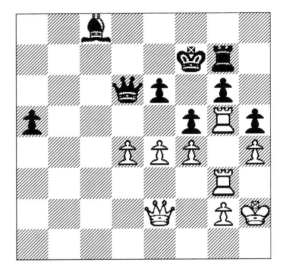

36. Rxg6! Rxg6 37. Qxh5 Qxf4 38. Qxg6+ and white wins.

Tal-Solmanis, Riga 1953

84

26) White to play

Black threatens to promote the a-pawn after a3-a2. **42. Rb7+** Kc3 43. Rb1 and white stops the dangerous passer. The Re7-e1 manoeuvre is also possible. But not 42. g5?? a2 43. Rb7+ Kc3 44. Rc7+ Kb2 45. Rb7+ Ka3 and black promotes, as the b1-square is controlled by the a2-pawn.

Tal-Straume, Riga 1953

27) White to play

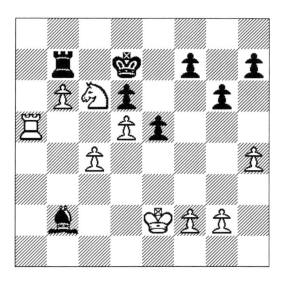

30. Ra7:
a) 30...Rxa7 31. bxa7 promotes
b) 30...Kc8 31. Ra8 Kd7 32. Rd8 mates

Tal-Darzniek, Riga 1953

28) Black to play

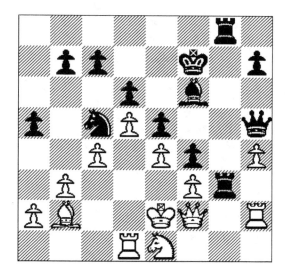

31...Nxe4! picks up a free pawn(32. Qa7 Ng5, attacking the f3-square).

Balin-Tal, Soviet Union 1953

29) White to play

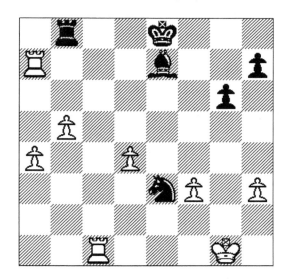

36. Rxe7+! Kxe7 37. Re1, followed by Rxe3 with sufficient material advantage.

Tal-Darznieks, Soviet Union 1953

31) White to play

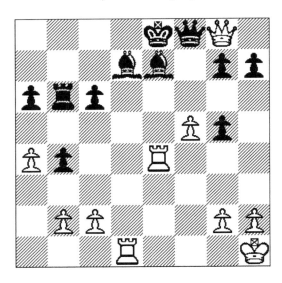

30) White to play

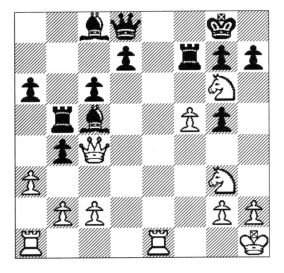

33. Rxe7+ Kxe7 34. Re1+ Kd6 35. Qxf8+

Tal-Kampenus, Soviet Union 1953

32) White to play

24. Nh8!(Ne5 is an alternative) d5 25. Nxf7 Kxf7 26. Qe2 and white should win. 25...dxc4 is weaker, because of 26. Nxd8.

Tal-Kampenus, Soviet Union 1953

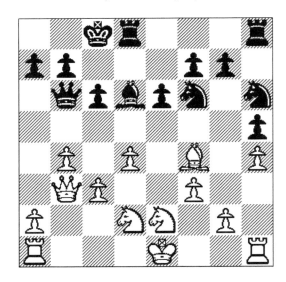

17. Nc4 Qc7 18. Nxd6 wins the exchange. An alternative is 17. Bxd6 Rxd6 18. Nc4, with a similar fork.

Tal-Rosenberg, Soviet Union 1953

33) Black to play

27...c3 28. bxc3 Qa3+ seals it(29. Kd1 Ne3+ 30. Ke1 Rxa2).

Melik-Tal, Leningrad 1954

34) Black to play

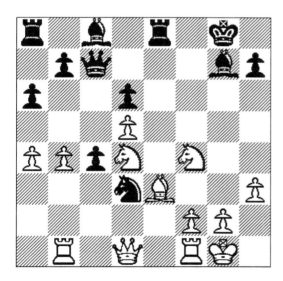

22...Bxd4 wins a piece:
a) 23. Bxd4 Nxf4
b) 23. Nxd3 Bxe3 24. fxe3 cxd3

Mileika-Tal, Riga 1954

35) White to play

36. Rxb5! Rxb5 37. Kxc4 Rc5+ 38. Kxd3 trades two pawns for the exchange, simplifying to a won rook endgame.

Tal-Etruk, Riga 1954

36) White to play

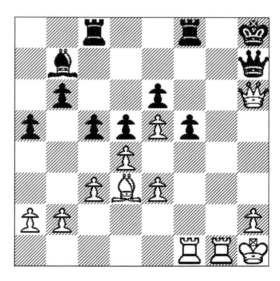

30. Qxh7+ Kxh7 31. Rf4 will deliver mate on h4.

Tal-Kliavins, Riga 1954

37) White to play

7. Nxe4 dxe4 8. Qa4+ forks the king and pawn on e4, winning a free pawn.

Tal-Liepin, Riga 1954

38) White to play

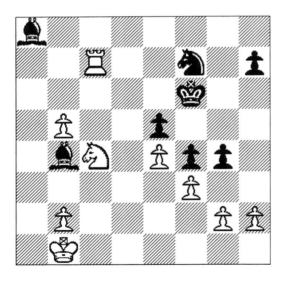

36. Ra7! now wins the trapped bishop. 36. Rc8 and 36. b6 are also good.

Tal-Visockiss, Riga 1954

39) Black to play

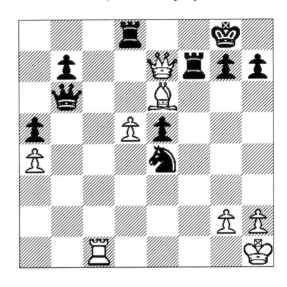

33...Nf2+! leads to a smothered mate, 34. Kg1 Nh3++ 35. Kh1 Qg1+! 36. Rxg1 Nf2#.

Vinokur-Tal, Riga 1954

40) Black to play

45...Be2!, attacking the rook, followed by f3-f2-f1, and black promotes. Other moves, like 45...d3, also win.

Prieditis-Tal, Soviet Union 1954

41) White to play

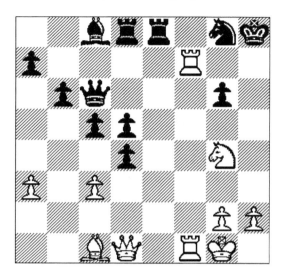

26. Qf3 threatens Qh3+ with an unavoidable mate in a number of moves.

Tal-Larichev, Soviet Union 1954

42) White to play

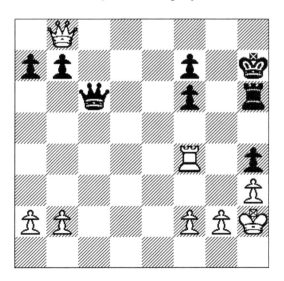

34. Rg4 Rg6 35. Rxh4+ Rh6 36. Rxh6+ Kxh6 37. Qh8+ Kg6 38. Qg8+ and Qxf7 wins two pawns.

Tal-Putjudrova, Latvia 1955

43) Black to play

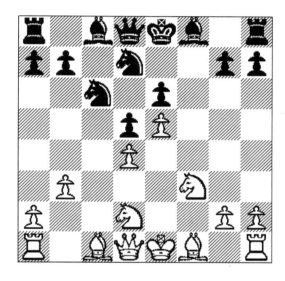

10...Nxd4! wins a pawn(Nxd4? Qh4+ and Qxd4)

Blek-Tal, Riga 1955

44) Black to play

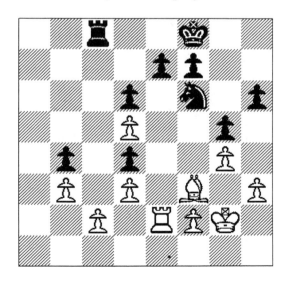

34...Rc5 and then Nxd5 wins a pawn.

Hanov-Tal, Riga 1955

45) White to play

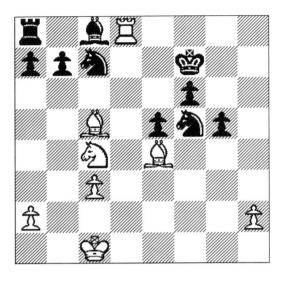

25. Rxc8! Rxc8 26. Bxf5 wins two minor pieces for rook, leaving white better.

Tal-Gipslis, Riga 1955

46) Black to play

43...Rg3!, threatening Rxf3 and Rf1+. On 44. Rc3, 44...Rg2 wins. 44. Rc8+ is impossible, because the queen guards the c8-square.

Lebedev-Tal, Riga 1955

47) Black to play

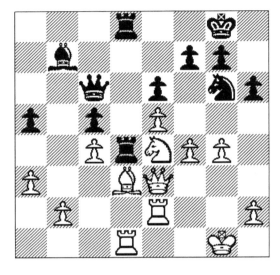

25...Rxe4 26. Qxe4 Qxe4 27. Bxe4 Rxd1+ wins a piece with additional big positional advantage.

Azerbaev-Tal, Soviet Union 1955

48) White to play

24...Qe6! is quite convincing after 25. Kf1 Qxe7 26. Qd2 Rxe1+ 27. Qxe1 Qxe1+ 28. Kxe1 Bxb2.
Black could have also lost the game after 24...Rxe3?? 25. Rxe3 and the e7-pawn promotes.

Rosenberg-Tal, Soviet Union 1955

49) White to play

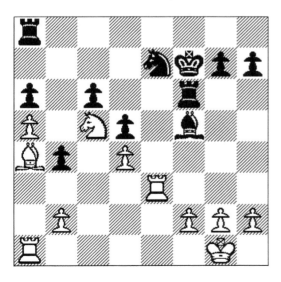

Although not the only way to a win, **27. Rb3** Rb8 28. Nxa6 Ra8 29. Nc5 Rxa5 30. Rxb4 picks up a pawn.

Tal-Neistadt, Soviet Union 1955

50) White to play

36. Rxg7+ Kh6 37. g5+ Kh5 38. gxf6 is extremely convincing.

Tal-Neistadt, Soviet Union 1955

51) Black to play

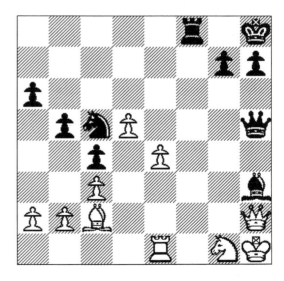

31...Bg2+! 32. Kxg2 Rf2+ 33. Kxf2 Qxh2+, followed by Qxc2, wins a lot of material.

Ostrauskas-Tal, Vilnius 1955

52) Black to play

16...Qb8! creates the double threat of capturing the pawns on b2 and h2 with check. One of those will fall.

Zhdanov-Tal, Vilnius 1955

53) Black to play

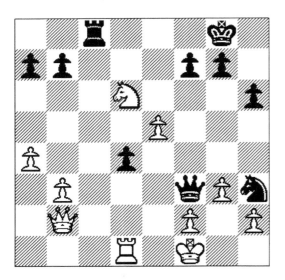

The quickest way to a win is **37...d3** 38. Ke1(mate in 1 after Qh1 has been threatening) Rc2.

Zvorykina-Tal, Vilnius 1955

54) Black to play

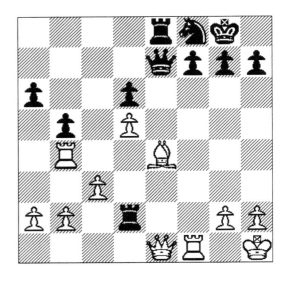

27...Rxd5! untraps the rook, while winning a pawn.

Khasin-Tal, Leningrad 1956

55) White to play

57. Rb4 will trade down rooks, with the ensuing 3 pawns versus knight ending easily won for the pawn side, as the pawns are very wide apart and the knight can not stop them.

Tal-Ragozin, Leningrad 1956

56) Black to play

27...**Qxa3+!** is mate in 2, 28. Kxa3/bxa3 Ra1#.

Chukaev-Tal, Tbilisi 1956

57) White to play

Although other moves, for example 35. Qxf7+, are also winning, **35. Qd3+** is most convincing, trading queens into a won pawn ending. After 35...Qxd3 36. Kxd3 Kg7 37. b4 the distant outside passer decides.

Tal-Yukhtman, Tbilisi 1956

58) White to play

93

38. Bxd5? Nxd5+ loses the pawn on b4. Correct is **38. Kd4!** Bxc4 39. Kxc4, winning a pawn, as 39...Nxa2? 40. Nd3! and Kb3 traps the black knight.

Tal-Barda, Uppsala 1956

59) Black to play

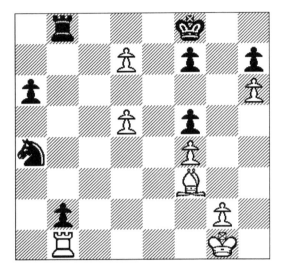

36...Ke7!, stopping the d7-passer, wins a whole rook after black plays Nc3 later. Huge blunder would be 36...Nc3?? instead, as after 37. Rxb2 black can not take on b2 with the rook because of 38. d8Q#, which leaves already white better.

Giustolisi-Tal, Italy 1957

60) Black to play

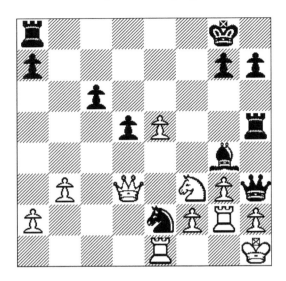

The easiest way to a win is **25...Nf4!**(26. gxf4 Bxf3).

Szabados-Tal, Italy 1957

61) White to play

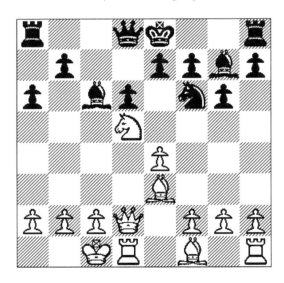

11. Bb6, attacking the queen, followed by Nc7+, wins the exchange on a8.

Tal-Ferrantes, Italy 1957

62) White to play

The discovered attack **25. Nxd5** wins a pawn.

Tal-Bronstein, Moscow 1957

63) White to play

46. Qe7+! Kg8 47. Qd8+ Kh7 48. Qxf6 Qe1+ 49. Kh2 forces black to sacrifice his queen on h4 to avoid immediate mate on g7.

Tal-Bronstein, Moscow 1957

64) Black to play

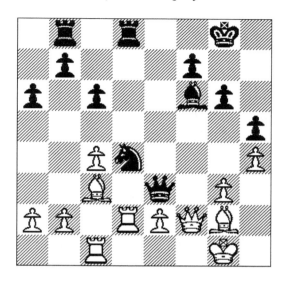

27...Nxe2+ 28. Rxe2 Qxc1+ wins the exchange.

Bannik-Tal, Moscow 1957

65) White to play

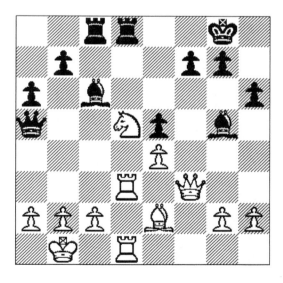

21. b4! Qa4/b5 22. Ra3 wins a lot of material due to the queen being trapped.

Tal-Larsen, Reykjavik 1957

66) White to play

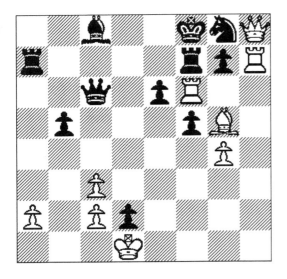

37. Qxg7+! Ke8 38. Rxf7 mates in a specific number of moves after the black checks end.

Tal-Koblents, Riga 1957

67) Black to play

31...b3! 32. axb3 a2 and now black threatens to continue with Rxf1. If 33. Bd4, then 33...Rd1. In case the white

light-square bishop moves, Rg1+, followed by a1Q+, wins.

Teschner-Tal, Vienna 1957

68) Black to play

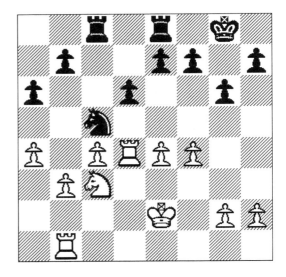

19...Ne6, followed by Nxf4, wins a free pawn.

Berhold-Tal, Munich 1958

69) Black to play

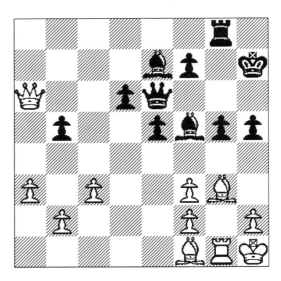

33...h4 wins the trapped bishop on g3.

Reissman-Tal, Munich 1958

70) White to play

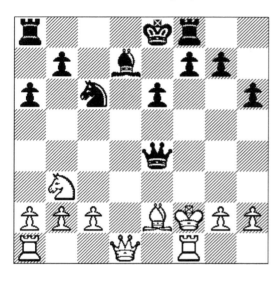

17. Qxd7+ Kxd7 18. Nc5+ and Nxe4 wins a whole piece.

Tal-Tringov, Munich 1958

71) Black to play

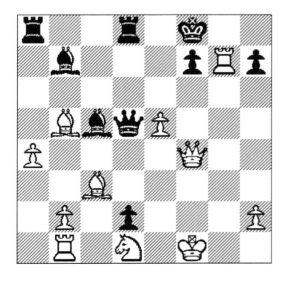

37...Qh1+ 38. Rg1 Qxg1+ 39. Ke2 Qe1#

Beni-Tal, Munich 1958

72) White to play

32. Qxh4?? Ke8 here is losing. **32. Qg7+!** Ke8 33. Qg8+ Kd7 34. Qxf7+ Kd6 35. Qe7+ Kd5 36. Qc5+ Ke4 37. Qe5# ends the game in 6.

Tal-Golombek, Munich 1958

73) Black to play

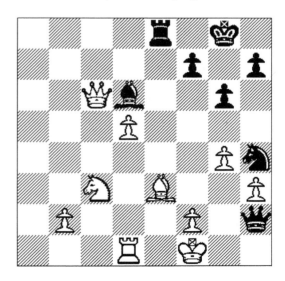

39...Rxe3! 40. Qc8+ Kg7 41. Qg8+ Kxg8 42. fxe3 Qg2+ 43. Ke1 Nf3# ends the struggle. 39...Qh1+ 40. Ke2 Qf3+ 41. Kd2 loses. 39...Qg2+ is identical.

Rossetto-Tal, Portoroz 1958

74) White to play

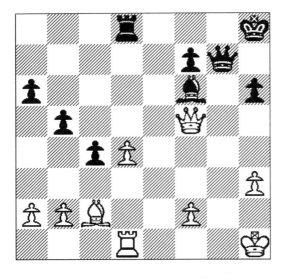

37. Rg1! Bg5(Qf8?? Qh7#) 38. f4 decides.

Tal-Filip, Portoroz 1958

75) Black to play

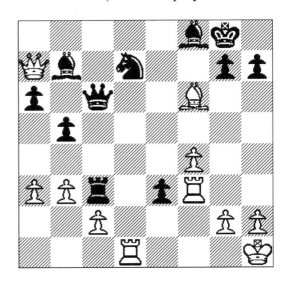

23...e2 24. Re1 Rxf3 ends the game.

Kliavins-Tal, Riga 1958

76) White to play

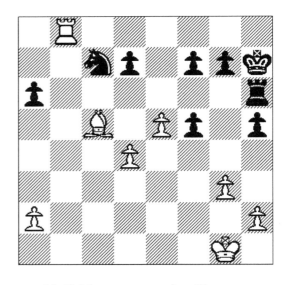

31. Rd8 recaptures the d7-pawn, although Stockfish gives this as fully equal. Other options like 31. Bd6 Nb5 or 31. Rb7 Rc6 might even slightly favour black.

Tal-Taimanov, Riga 1958

77) White to play

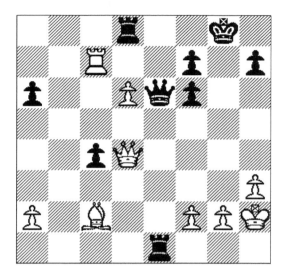

26. Re7! wins:
a) 26...Qxd6 27. Qxd6 Rxd6 28. Rxe1
b) 26...Qxe7 27. Qg4+!(but not 27. dxe7?? Rxd4), unpinning the queen, and then dxe7

Tal-Geller, Riga 1958

78) White to play

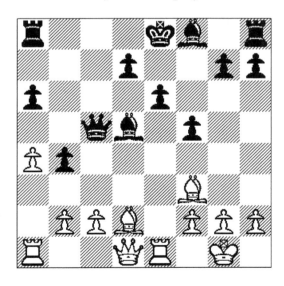

16. Bxd5 Qxd5 is about equal. The correct solution is **16. Bxb4!** and now:

a) 16...Qxb4 17. Qxd5 Rd8 18. Qe5 and the king in the center and lack of development make defence impossible for black
b) 16...Bxf3 17. Qxf3 Qc8 18. Bc3 is hopeless too

Tal-Gipslis, Riga 1958

79) White to play

The winning tactic is **24. Rxd7!** Qxd7 25. Qxa8+ Kf7 26. fxe6+ Rxe6 27. Rxe6 Qxe6 28. Qf3+ and black is hopeless.

Tal-Gipslis, Riga 1958

80) Black to play

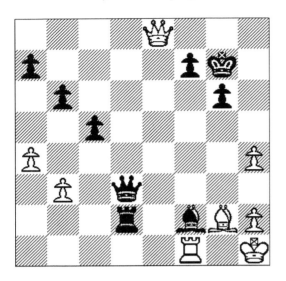

35...Rd1 and white has no defence, 36.
Qe5+ Kh7.

Averbakh-Tal, Riga 1958

81) Black to play

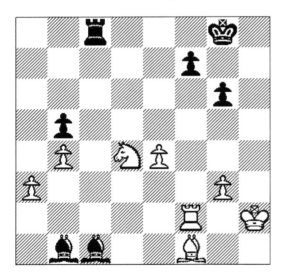

41...Be3! 42. Rb2 Rc1!, attacking the
f1-bishop, wins a piece.

Klasup-Tal, Soviet Union 1958

82) Black to play

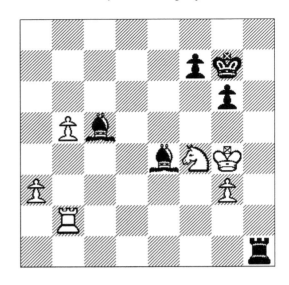

The shortest way to a win is **51...f5+**
52. Kg5 Be7#.

Klasup-Tal, Soviet Union 1958

83) Black to play

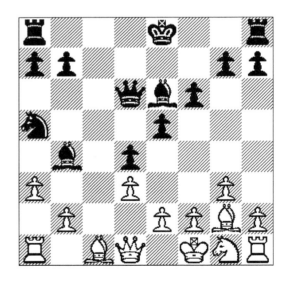

15...Bb3! wins the queen.

Peterson-Tal, Soviet Union 1958

84) White to play

21. Qg5! threatens Qh6+ with an unavoidable mate. The only other clearly winning move is 21. f5, otherwise black might try to hold after Rg8.

Tal-Kampenus, Soviet Union 1958

85) White to play

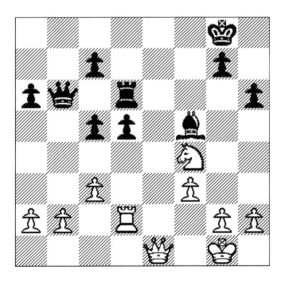

27. Nxd5 seals it:
a) if the queen retreats, Ne7+ and Nxf5 wins

b) 27...Rxd5 28. Rxd5
c) 27...Re6 28. Qh4!, renewing the same threat, Ne7+ and Nxf5; on 28...Qd6 29. Nf6+ and Rxd6 wins

Tal-Klovans, Soviet Union 1958

86) White to play

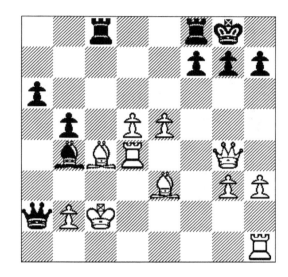

25. Bh6! Rxc4+(g6 Bxf8 is hopeless) 26. Rxc4 Qxc4+ 27. Qxc4 bxc4 28. Bf4 gives white excellent winning chances due to the strong pawn center.

Tal-Mileika, Soviet Union 1958

101

87) White to play

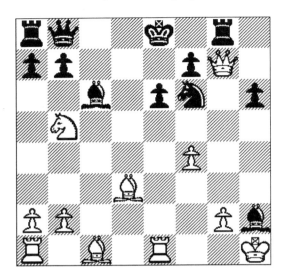

19. Rxe6+! fxe6(19...Kd8 20. Qxf6+
Kc8 21. Qxf7 makes no distinction) 20.
Bg6+ Kd8 21. Qxf6+ Kd7 22. Qf7+
Kd8 23. Qxg8+ Ke7 24. Qf7+ Kd8 25.
Qf8+ mates.

Tal-Nei, Soviet Union 1958

88) White to play

32. Qxf8+ Kg6 33. Qg8+ Kf5(Kh6
Qg7#) 34. Ng7+! and Qxc4 wins the
queen.

Tal-Portisch, Varna 1958

89) Black to play

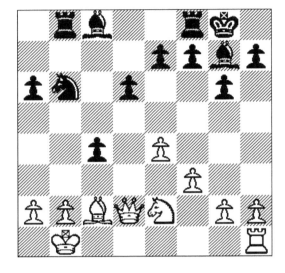

Easily winning is **20...c3!** and now:
a) 21. Qd3 cxb2, and the newly created
powerful passer will decide the game
b) 21. Nxc3 Nc4! 22. Qe1 Rxb2+ 23.
Kc1 Bh6+! 24. Kd1 Ne3+ might be
even worse

Bobotsov-Tal, Varna 1958

102

90) Black to play

29...Rc1+ 30. Rxc1 Rxc1+ seals it.

Bobotsov-Tal, Varna 1958

91) Black to play

44...d3! wins on the spot:
a) 45. Bxd3 Rxd3 46. Rxd3 e2 47.
Rge3 e1Q+ 48. Rxe1 Rxe1+ leaves
black a piece up
b) 45. Rxd3 Rxd3 46. Bxd3 e2 is even
worse

Olafsson-Tal, Bled 1959

92) Black to play

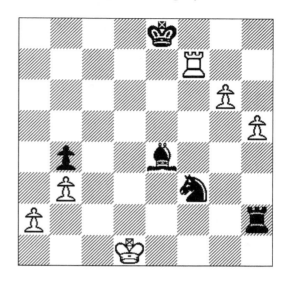

71...Bd3 threatens Rh1#. If 72. Rxf3,
then 72...Be2+ and Bxf3.

Olafsson-Tal, Bled 1959

93) Black to play

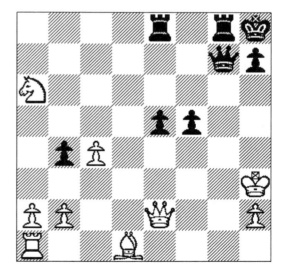

33...Re6, threatening Rh6+, decides.
33...Qh6+ is an alternative.

Fischer-Tal, Bled 1959

94) White to play

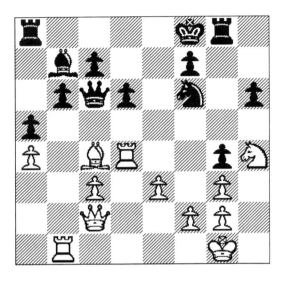

24. Bb5 Qc5 25. Rc4, followed by Rxc7, when the queen retreats, wins back the pawn, leaving white with a superior position.

Tal-Gligoric, Bled 1959

95) White to play

60. f5! Kxa1 61. f6 Kb1 62. fxe7 a1Q 63. e8Q should win for white.

Tal-Gligoric, Bled 1959

96) Black to play

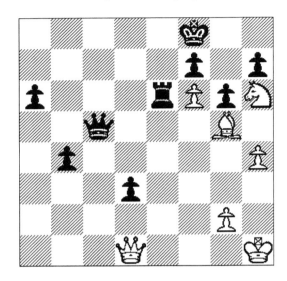

38...Qc2 39. Qf3 d2 40. Bxd2 Qxd2 wins.

Keres-Tal, Bled 1959

97) White to play

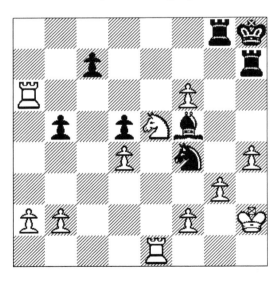

36. gxf4?? Rh4#. Winning is **36. f7!** Rf8 and only now 37. gxf4, winning back the minor piece.

Tal-Olafsson, Bled 1959

98) White to play

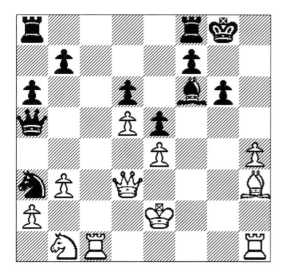

23. b4! Qxb4/Qd8 24. Nxa3 wins a
minor piece.

Tal-Gligoric, Bled 1959

99) White to play

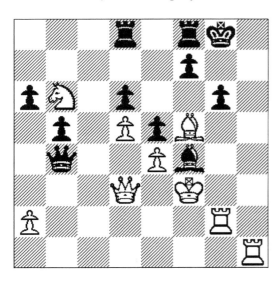

31. Nd7 Kg7 32. Nxf8 Rxf8 leaves
white a whole rook up. 31...Rc8 32.
Bxg6! fxg6 33. Rxg6+ Kf7 34. Rf6+ is
weaker.

Tal-Gligoric, Bled 1959

100) White to play

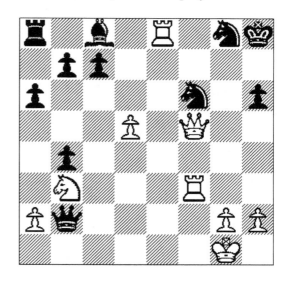

28. Qxf6+ Qxf6 29. Rxf6 ends the
struggle

Tal-Fischer, Bled 1959

101) Black to play

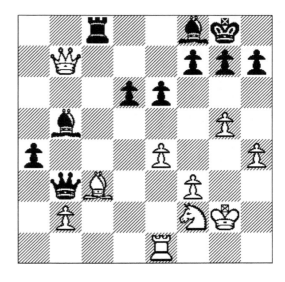

33...Bf1+! wins the queen on b7.

Benko-Tal, Bled 1959

102) Black to play

32...Rxf4+ 33. Kg2 fxg4 ensures black large advantage.

Gligoric-Tal, Bled 1959

103) Black to play

Other moves might win too, but **51...Ba1!**, clearing the road forward for the b-pawn, while still defending the

rook, followed by b2, is the most convincing approach.

Fischer-Tal, Bled 1959

104) White to play

41. Rd7+ Nxd7 42. Rxd7+ Kg8 43. a7 decides.

Tal-Olafsson, Bled 1959

105) White to play

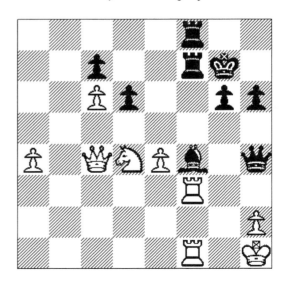

Tal played here **36. Rxf4**, but 36. Ne6+ also wins.

Tal-Fischer, Bled 1959

106) Black to play

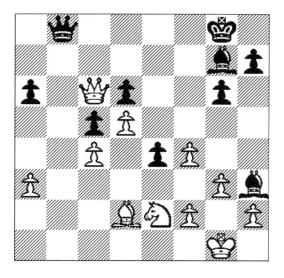

29...Qb1+ 30. Bc1/Nc1 Qc2 31. Qe8+ Bf8 and the back rank mate is preventable, only if white sacrifices his queen on e6.

Benko-Tal, Bled 1959

107) Black to play

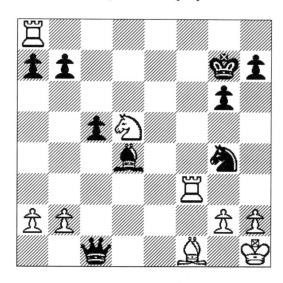

26...Nf2+ 27. Kg1 Ne4+ 28. Kh1 Ng3+! is a sudden mate, 29. hxg3 Qh6#, or 29. Rxg3 Qxf1#.

Niemela-Tal, Riga 1959

108) White to play

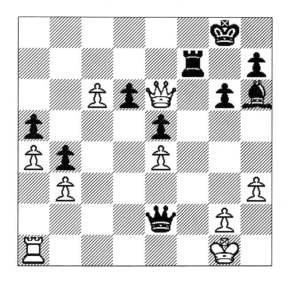

37. c7 Kg7 38. c8Q Be3+ 39. Kh2! Bf4+ 40. Kh1 wins. In above line, 39. Kh1?? instead is a big mistake, as black mates with 39...Rf1+

Tal-Dauga, Riga 1959

109) White to play

23. Bxe6+? Rxe6 is a mistake. **23. Qc7** Rxd7 24. Qxd7 wins.

Tal-Franz, Riga 1959

110) White to play

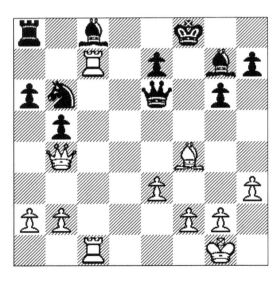

Most convincing is **25. Rxe7!** and now:
a) 25...Qxe7 26. Bd6
b) 25...Nd5 26. Rxe6+ Nxb4 27. Bc5+ Kf7 28. Re7+ and Bxb4

c) 25...a5 26. Qc5 Qd5 27. Qc7

Tal-Johannessen, Riga 1959

111) White to play

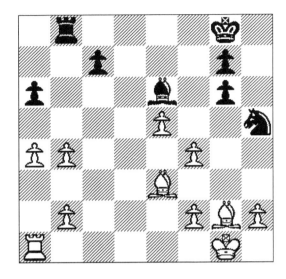

30. b5! seals it. After 30...axb5 31. a5, or 30...a5 31. Rc1 the advanced white pawns will soon promote.

Tal-Witkowski, Riga 1959

112) Black to play

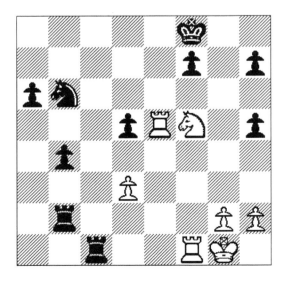

Other moves also win, but best is
38...Rbb1! and now:
a) 39. Ne3 d4
b) 39. Rxc1 Rxc1+ 40. Kf2 b3 41. Re2
Rc2 and the b-pawn is unstoppable

Tolush-Tal, Riga 1959

114) Black to play

Most convincing is **37...Nxa2!**,
winning another pawn. 38. Bxa2? b3
39. Bb1 a3 and black promotes.

Kliavins-Tal, Riga 1959

115) White to play

113) Black to play

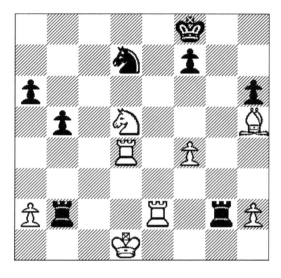

25...Rg1+! 26. Re1 Rb1+ 27. Kd2
Rbxe1 wins a whole rook.

Kliavins-Tal, Riga 1959

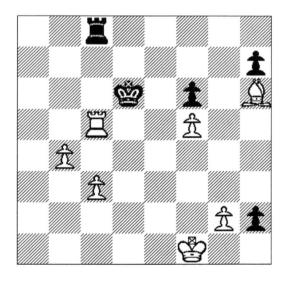

43. Rxc8?? h1Q+ is a huge blunder. **43.
Bf4+** and Bxh2 wins.

Tal-Bronstein, Tbilisi 1959

116) White to play

Black threatens to promote at any time after Nf3+ and e2-e1. 52. Nxe3?? is weak, because of 52...Rxd2 53. Kc5 Rxd6 54. Kxd6 Rxe3. Therefore, the only correct approach is **52. Re6+**, followed by a capture on e3, and the dangerous black passed pawn is gone.

Tal-Gurgenidze, Tbilisi 1959

117) White to play

66. c8Q wins:
a) 66...Nxc8 67. Nd5+ and Nxf4
b) 66...Rxc4+ 67. Qxc4

Tal-Gurgenidze, Tbilisi 1959

118) White to play

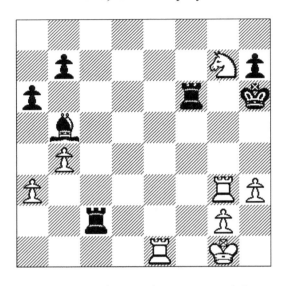

32. Re5!, threatening mate on h5, 32...Rc1+ 33. Kh2 Rg6 34. Nf5+ Kh5 35. Ne7+ Kh6 36. Nxg6 hxg6 37. Re6 decides.

Tal-Polugaevsky, Tbilisi 1959

119) Black to play

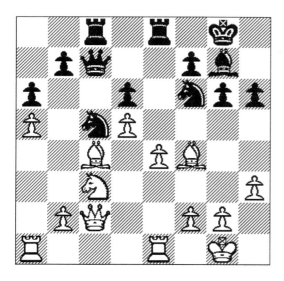

19...Nfxe4 20. Nxe4 Nxe4 21. Rxe4 Rxe4 22. Qxe4 Qxc4 23. Qxc4 Rxc4 is slightly better for black. Alternatives favour white, who keeps the bishop pair and stronger pawn center.

Geller-Tal, Tbilisi 1959

120) White to play

75. Rxf6! Rxh6+ 76. Rxh6+ Qxh6+ 77. Qh3 leads to a winning pawn endgame. 75...Qxf6? 76. Qc8+ is mate.

Tal-Krogius, Tbilisi 1959

121) White to play

22. Bxh6! gxh6 23. Ne4 compromises the black pawn structure and posts an excellent central knight. After that, white is very close to winning.

Tal-Brakmanis, Soviet Union 1959

122) White to play

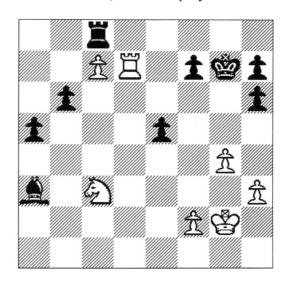

33. Nb5, followed by Rd8, wins a rook. 33. Nd5 is an alternative.

Tal-Brakmanis, Soviet Union 1959

123) White to play

Other moves also win, but **39. Kg3!**, cutting the access to the f4-square for the black king, will deliver mate on the next move with Rg7.

Tal-Brakmanis, Soviet Union 1959

124) White to play

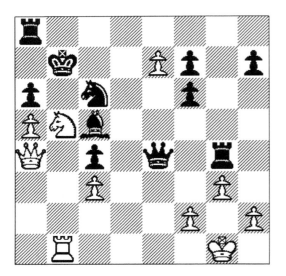

26. Nd6++ Kc7 27. Nxe4 Rxe4 28. Kg2 leaves white better, as, although black has material advantage, all black pieces are tangled up and the black pawns weak.

Tal-Keller, Zurich 1959

125) White to play

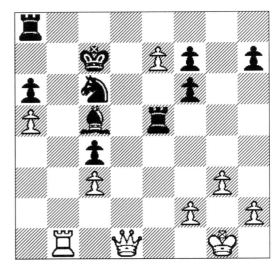

29. Rb7+! Kxb7 30. Qd7+ Kb8 31. e8Q+ Rxe8 32. Qxe8+ Kb7 33. Qd7+ Kb8 34. Qxc6 ends the game.

Tal-Keller, Zurich 1959

126) Black to play

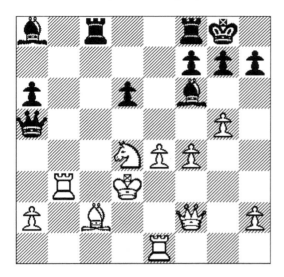

24...Bxd4 ends the struggle:
a) 25. Qxd4 Qxe1
b) 25. Kxd4 Qc5+ and Qxf2

Jupper-Tal, Zurich 1959

127) White to play

43. e5+ is the final touch:
a) 43...dxe5 44. Kxc5
b) 43...Kxf5 44. Nd4+ and Nxb3
c) 43...Kg7 44. e6 and the white passers
are unstoppable

Tal-Duckstein, Zurich 1959

128) Black to play

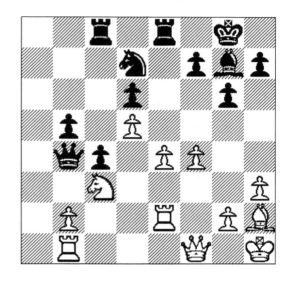

24...Bxc3 25. bxc3 Qxc3 creates a
dangerous passed pawn.

Donner-Tal, Zurich 1959

129) White to play

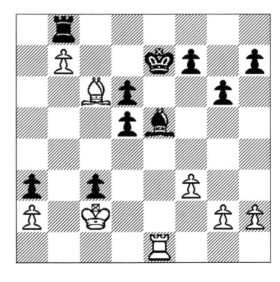

32. f4 wins the black bishop.

Tal-Larsen, Zurich 1959

130) White to play

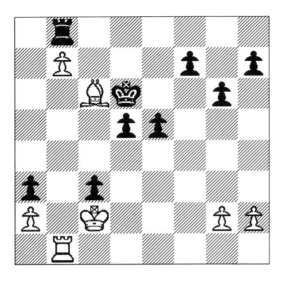

35. Rb6! Kc7 36. Ra6 is the most efficient way to win, while defending the bishop. 35. Be8 also wins. On the other hand, 35. Ba4? d4 is just a draw.

Tal-Larsen, Zurich 1959

131) Black to play

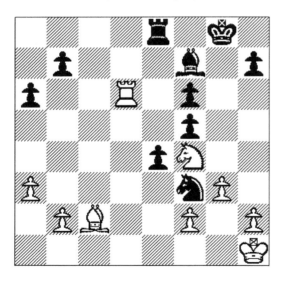

30...Rc8! 31. Bd1 Rc1 activates the rook, while pinning the opponent

bishop, which should guarantee an easy win.

Unzicker-Tal, Zurich 1959

132) Black to play

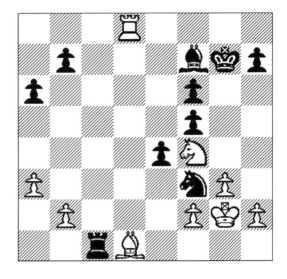

33...Ne1+ 34. Kh3 Nd3 35. Be2 Nxf4+ 36. gxf4 Rc2 is hopeless. In above line, 34. Kf1 Nd3 35. Ke2 Nxb2 is even weaker.

Unzicker-Tal, Zurich 1959

133) White to play

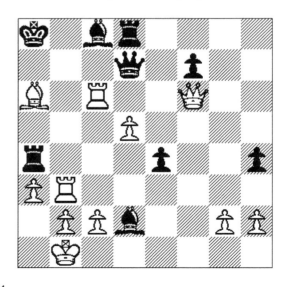

114

Best is **37. Bxc8** Rxc8 38. Ra6+ Qa7 39. Rxa7 Rxa7 40. d6 and white wins.

Tal-Nievergelt, Zurich 1959

134) White to play

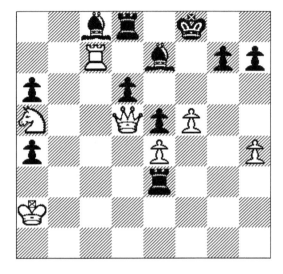

31. Nc6 Re8(black can also give couple of spite checks) 32. Nxe7 ends the game.

Tal-Stoltz, Teleschach 1959

135) White to play

40. Rg7+! Kf8 41. Rh7, threatening mate on h8, 41...Kg8 42. Rh1 and white stops the dangerous e-passer and later should be able to convert.

Tal-Teschner, Hamburg 1960

136) Black to play

21...Qa1+ 22. Ke2 Re8+ seals it.

Troger-Tal, Hamburg 1960

137) White to play

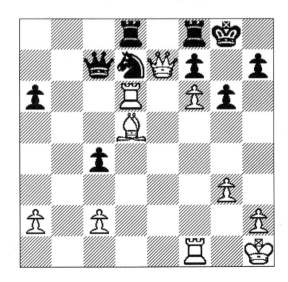

27. Rd1 and, after the bishop retreats, the pin decides.

Tal-Darga, Hamburg 1960

138) Black to play

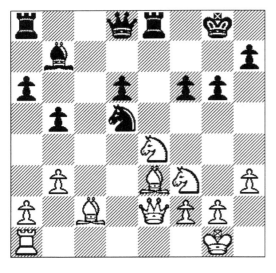

24...Nxe3 25. Qxe3 Bxe4 26. Bxe4 d5 wins a piece.

Unzicker-Tal, Hamburg 1960

139) White to play

Other moves win too, but **34. Rxg5+!** Nxg5 35. Bxg5 f3 36. Bh3, followed by d7, is most convincing.

Tal-Padevsky, Leipzig 1960

140) White to play

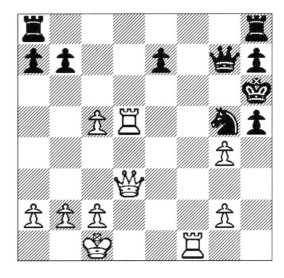

27. Rh1, intending Rxh5+, ends the game.

Tal-Campomanes, Leipzig 1960

141) Black to play

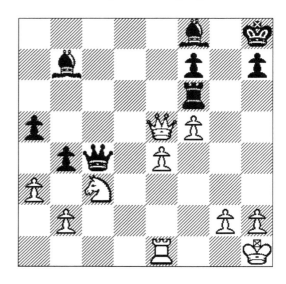

After **29...Qa6!** 30. axb4 axb4 31. Nd5 Bxd5 32. exd5 h5 black has no problems winning. 29...Qc6? instead is a mistake, which after 30. Nd5 Bg7 31. Qb8+ leaves white winning.

Durao-Tal, Leipzig 1960

142) White to play

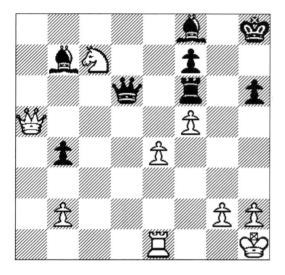

35...Bxe4! is the last touch. The bishop is uncapturable, because of Qd1+, and on 36. Ne8, black has 36...Qd2 37. Rg1 Rxf5.

Durao-Tal, Leipzig 1960

Intermediate Tal

143) White to play

17. Bxh7+!! Kxh7 18. Rh3+, checking sequences frequently lead to mate in similar situations, Kg8 19. Nf5!(Qh5? f5) Qg5(Qe8 Qh5 f6 Qh7+ Kf7 Qxg7#) 20. Qh5!! and Tal's opponent resigned here because of 20...Qxh5 21. Ne7+ Kh7 22. Rxh5#

It should be noted that black could have survived with only heavy material loss after 19...exf5 20. Qxe7, picking up the loose queen.

Tal-NN, Exhibition 1949

144) Black to play

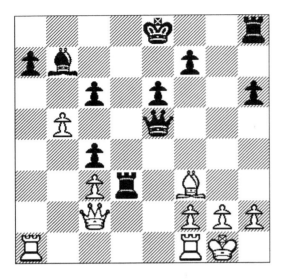

18...Rxf3! leads to a forced win:
a) 19. gxf3? Rg8+ 20. Kh1 cxb5, opening the a8-h1 diagonal, 21. Qd1 Qf4, followed by a deadly bishop check on f3
b) 19. Rxa7 Qb8 20. Rxb7 Qxb7 21. gxf3 cxb5 and black has winning advantage

Kholmov-Tal, Riga 1949

145) Black to play

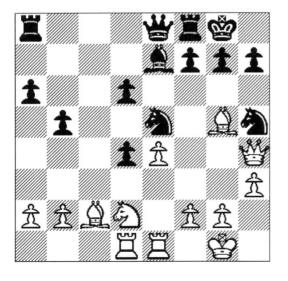

19...f6! protects the knight on h5 with the queen and threatens the bishop on g5. All options are losing:
a) 20. Bf4 g5 is a fork
b) 20. g4 fxg5 21. Qxh5 Qd7 and black traps and captures white's queen after g6 Qh6, Kh8 and Nf7; if white plays Bb3 not to allow Nf7, then the d3 square remains unprotected and black wins after Nd3-f4, this time trapping the queen on h5

Parnas-Tal, Riga 1949

146) White to play

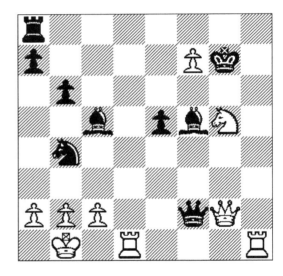

26. Ne6++ a deadly double check leads to a long, but fully forced, mate, 26...Kxf7 27. Qg7+ Kxe6 28. Rh6+! Bg6 29. Qxg6+ Ke7 30. Rh7+ Kf8 31. Qg7+ Ke8 32. Qd7+ Kf8 33. Rh8#

Tal-Zilber, Riga 1949

147) Black to play

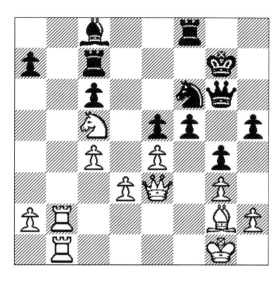

30...f4! 31. gxf4 Qh6!(pinning the f4 pawn to the loose queen on e3) 32. Rf1 Nh7 and then exf4 creates couple of very powerful passed storming pawns that will decide the game.

Julik-Tal, Riga 1950

148) Black to play

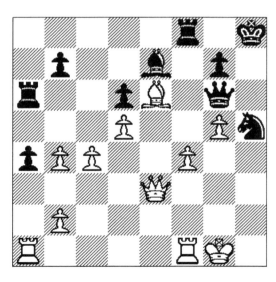

29...Nxf4! wins another pawn. 30. Rxf4 is impossible, as 30...Qxg5+ is a double attack on king and rook(Rg4 Qxe3+).

Liepin-Tal, Riga 1950

149) Black to play

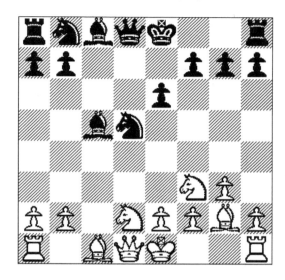

8...Bxf2+!! 9. Kxf2 Qb6+ 10. Ke1 Ne3 forks the queen on d1 and bishop on g2. Black returns the piece, staying with a pawn more.

Pakala-Tal, Riga 1950

150) Black to play

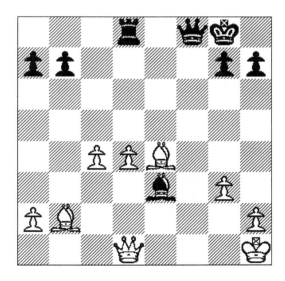

25...Qf2!, attacking the bishop on b2. After the bishop retreats, black captures the important central d4-pawn.

Berg-Tal, Riga 1951

151) Black to play

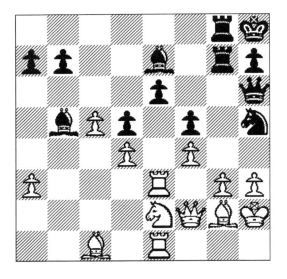

30...Nxg3! 31. Nxg3 Bh4! wins black material due to the nasty pin on the knight.

Birjanis-Tal, Riga 1951

152) Black to play

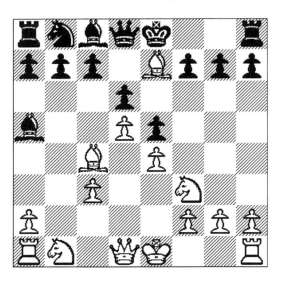

Black has to recapture on e7. Currently, if white were to move, he could deliver a forking check on a4, but, in reply, c7-c6 simultaneously interposes a pawn, while defending the bishop on a5 with the queen. If black captures on e7 with the queen, Qa4+ already wins the bishop. **9...Kxe7!**, the right move, leaving black with some advantage.

Klovans-Tal, Riga 1951

153) White to play

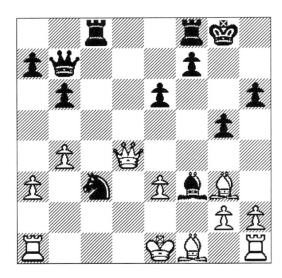

22. Qf6! is the correct move, followed by 23. Qxf3, winning a piece. Black can not move the bishop, as Be5, creating a battery, with an unavoidable mate on g7 threatens. 22. gxf3 instead is a huge blunder, as after 22...Qxf3 23. Rg1 Rfd8 24. Qe5 Rd5! the white queen is lost(25. Bg2?? Qe2#).

Tal-Gipslis, Riga 1951

120

154) White to play

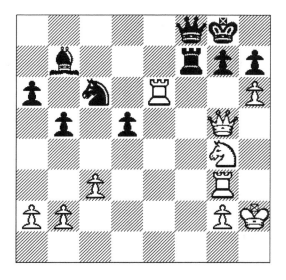

Tal found here the mate in 9 after 34. Re8! Qxe8 35. Nf6+ Kf8 36. hxg7+. **34. hxg7!** Rxg7 35. Nh6+ Kh8 36. Qxg7+! Qxg7 37. Re8+ is mate in 5. Maybe Tal picked the more attractive solution?

Tal-Veder, Riga 1951

155) White to play

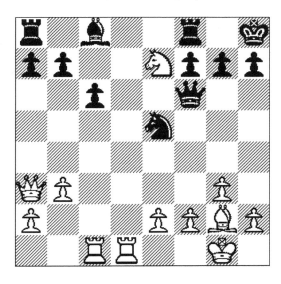

21. Nd5!, threatening the queen and rook on f8, wins white a whole rook

after 21...Qd8 22. Nc7!(a second discovered attack upon the queen with the same motif) and 23. Nxa8, as capturing the knight on both occasions is impossible because of Qxf8#. Please, note, that 21. Ng6+?? is a blunder(21...Nxg6 protects the rook).

Tal-Birjanis, Riga 1952

156) White to play

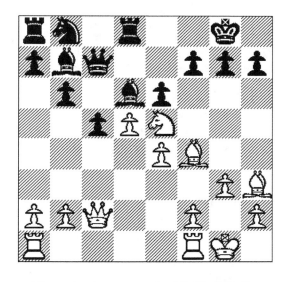

The winning move is **16. Nxf7!**, for example:
a) 16...Qxf7 17. Bxe6
b) 16...Kxf7 17. Bxe6+ Kf8 18. e5!, followed by Qxh7
c) 16...Bxf4 17. Nxd8

Tal-Lozov, Riga 1952

121

157) White to play

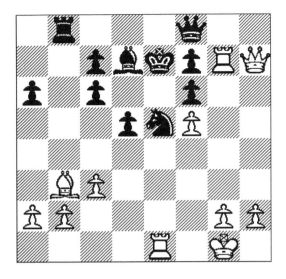

30. Rxe5+! is quick and efficient. After the forced line 30...fxe5 31. Qh4+ Kd6(Ke8 Qg5, threatening a pin on g8) 32. Qf6+ Kc5 33. Rxf7 white has huge advantage.

Tal-Zhdanov, Soviet Union 1952

158) White to play

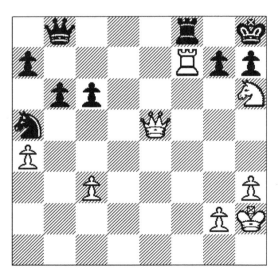

Qxg7 mate is impossible, because the queen is pinned. Here Tal played 40. Rc7!, which is winning after 40...Rf6

41. Qe7 Qf8 42. Qd7 Rxh6 43. Rc8 Rf6 44. Rxf8 Rxf8 45. Qxa7
Tal missed a great finish, though, available after the quiet **40. g3!!** Rg8(Qxe5 Rf8#) 41. Rxg7! Rxg7(Qxe5 Rxg8#) 42. Qxb8+ Rg8 43. Qxg8# Tal is not Stockfish after all.

Tal-Zwaigzne, Soviet Union 1952

159) White to play

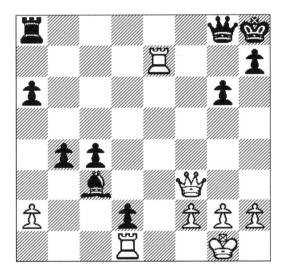

32. Rxd2! gets rid of the dangerous d2-passer. Recapturing is impossible because of Qf6+ with mate to follow. After 32...Rf8 33. Qe4 Bf6 34. Rdd7 b3 35. axb3 cxb3 36. Rxh7+ Qxh7 37. Rxh7+ Kxh7 38. Qb7+ and Qxb3 white is winning.

Tal-Maslov, Kharkov 1953

122

160) White to play

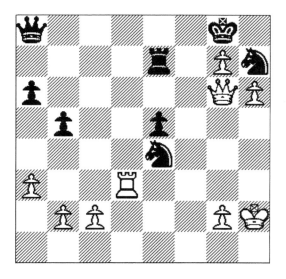

34. Qxe4! and the two white advanced connected passers are much stronger than the stranded black knight on h7. In case of a queen recapture, 34...Qxe4, 35. Rd8+ Kf7 36. g8Q+ Kf6 37. Rd6+ Kf5 38. Qg6+ Kf4 39. g3+ Ke3 40. Rd3+ wins.

Tal-Pasman, Latvia 1953

161) White to play

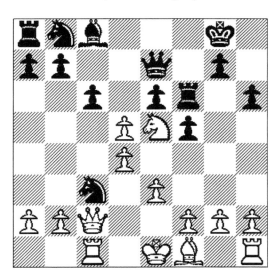

After the natural recapture 13. Qxc3 exd5 black is fine. **13. d6!**, an important intermediate move, which after 13...Qxd6 14. Qxc3 compromises the black pawn structure(less central pawns), while leaving the c8-bishop less active.

Tal-Solmanis, Riga 1953

162) Black to play

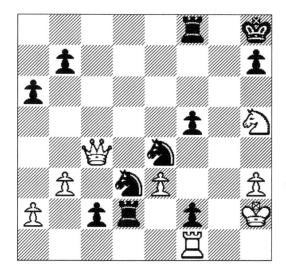

33...c1Q! and black wins:
a) 34. Qxc1 Nxc1
b) 34. Rxc1 f1Q#
c) 34. Qd4+ Nf6 35. Nxf6 Qb2
33...Rd1 is a mistake, as after 34. Qd4+ Nf6 35. Qd6!(attacking the rook on f8) Rf7 36. Qd8+ Ng8 37. Qd4+ white has a perpetual.

Udris-Tal, Riga 1953

123

163) Black to play

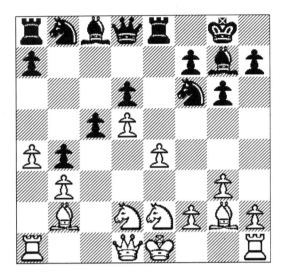

12...Nxe4! is more than convincing:
a) 13. Nxe4 Bxb2
b) 13. Bxg7 Nxd2 14. Qxd2 Kxg7; in this line, 14. Bh6 is weaker, because of 14...Bg4(attacking e2) 15. Be3 Nf3+

Mileika-Tal, Soviet Union 1953

164) Black to play

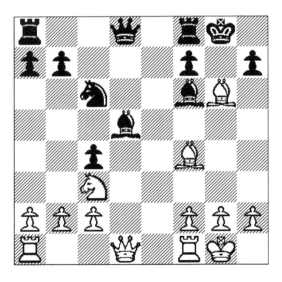

White has just captured on g6.
15...Bxc3! 16. Bxh7+ Kxh7 17. Qh5+ Kg8 18. bxc3 Qf6 19. Qg4+ Qg6

successfully repels the attack, keeping a piece more. 15...hxg6 16. Nxd5, on the other hand, leaves white better.

Akmentin-Tal, Riga 1954

165) Black to play

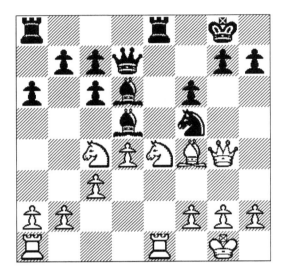

19...Rxe4!(Bxe4 is an alternative) 20. Rxe4 Bxe4 21. Bxd6(a discovered attack upon the e4-bishop) Bd5!(an intermediate move, attacking the knight on c4) 22. Ne3 Be6!(threatening a discovered attack on the queen after Nxe3 capture) wins a piece in an elegant way. A huge blunder would be 19...Bxc4?? instead, allowing 20. Nxf6+ royal fork.

Gufeld-Tal, Riga 1954

166) White to play

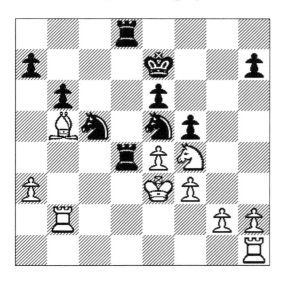

27. Nd5+!, severing the connection between the two rooks, wins the exchange for pawn, leaving white clearly better after 27...R4xd5 28. exd5. 27...exd5 28. Kxd4 is weaker, as the knight on e5 is attacked.

Tal-Etruk, Riga 1954

167) White to play

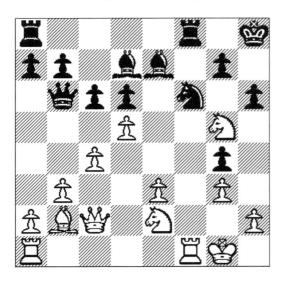

According to the records of the game, white played here 18. Rxf6?, which

after 18...Qe3+!(an important intermediate move) 19. Kg2 Qxg5 20. Rg6 Qf5 21. Qxf5 Bxf5 22. Rxg7 Bf6 23. Bxf6 Rxf6 24. Rxb7 leads just to a minimal edge, closer to a draw. Using the very same motif, the right move has been **18. Bd4!**(defending the e3-pawn and preparing Rxf6) hxg5 19. Bxb6 and white wins. If 18...c5?, then 19. Rxf6!! already crashes through:
a) 19...Bxf6 20. Qh7#
b) 19...hxg5 20. Rh6+ Kg8 21. Qh7+ Kf7 22. Qg6+!(not allowing the king to escape via e8) Kg8 23. Qxg7#

Tal-Semenkin, Riga 1954

168) Black to play

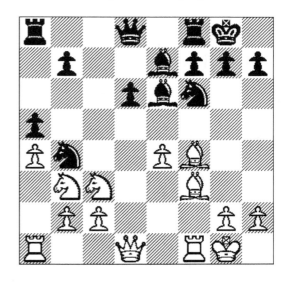

13...Nxc2! 14. Qxc2 Qb6+, followed by Bxb3, wins an important pawn.

Vinokur-Tal, Riga 1954

169) White to play

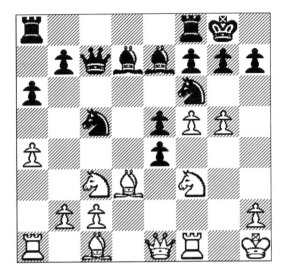

16. gxf6 wins a piece:
a) 16...Bxf6 17. Nxe4
b) 16...exd3/exf3 17. fxe7

Tal-Saigin, Riga 1954

170) Black to play

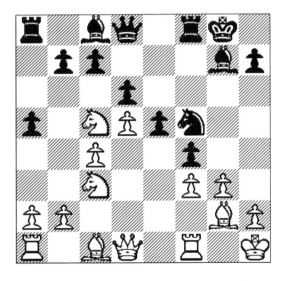

18...Nxg3+! is very effective and efficient at the same time:
a) 19. Kg1 Nxf1 wins the exchange

b) 19. hxg3? is even more convincing for black after 19...fxg3 20. Kg1(Qh4+ threatens) Qh4 21. Re1 Qh2+ 22. Kf1 Bh3 23. Ke2(Bxh3 Qf2#) Qxg2+, winning in style
18...dxc5 19. g4 is just better for black.

Niebult-Tal, Soviet Union 1954

171) Black to play

29...Be4 seals it:
a) 30. Bd3 Qf5!(both 30...Bxd3? 31. Re8+! and 30...Rxd3? 31. Rxd3 are mistakes, leaving white better) 31. Bxe4 Rxd2 32. Rxd2 Qg5 33. Rxd8+ Nxd8 and black should win
b) 30. Rxe4 is even weaker, for example 30...Qxe4 31. Qxd6 Rxd6 32. Rxd6 Qb1+ and Qxb2
Black could also have lost after a careless move like 29...h5, as 30. Re8+! wins the queen on f4.

Pasman-Tal, Soviet Union 1954

126

172) White to play

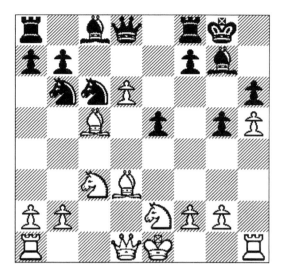

16. d7! Bxd7 17. Bxf8 Qxf8 18. 0-0 Rd8 19. Qb1 keeps for white a tiny edge. White certainly can not hope for more in other lines.

Tal-Shianovsky, Riga 1955

173) Black to play

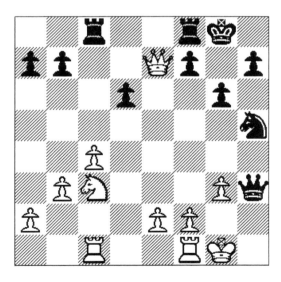

18...Nxg3! 19. hxg3 Qxg3+ 20. Kh1 Rce8 21. Qxb7 Qh4+! 22. Kg1 Re5 and black wins:

a) 23. Qg2 Rg5, pinning the queen
b) 23. Rf2 Qg5+, forking the king and the already undefended rook on c1
Tal played the weaker 21...Re5, which still wins pretty convincingly.

Bannik-Tal, Riga 1955

174) Black to play

49...Na4+! mates in a number of moves:
a) 50. bxa4 Rb7+! 51. Ka3(51. Kc3 Qd4#) Qxb1
b) 50. Ka2(Ka3 and Ka1 are identical) Nc3++ 51. Kb2 Ra2+ 52. Kxc3 Qd4#

Chukayev-Tal, Riga 1955

175) White to play

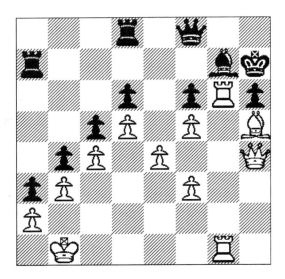

40. Rxg7+! Other moves also win, but this tactical continuation is very forceful and convincing. After 40...Rxg7 41. Bg6+ Kg8 42. Qxh6 Qe7 43. Kc1!(so that black does not have check on e4 after f3-f4) Rd7 44. Rh1 Kf8 45. f4 and e5 the end is clear.

Tal-Solovyev, Riga 1955

176) White to play

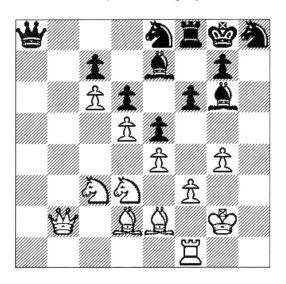

29. Ra1 Qd8 30. Qb7!, followed by Ra8, wins the queen.

Tal-Kudriashov, Soviet Union 1955

177) White to play

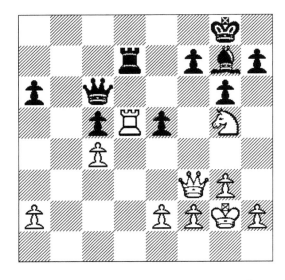

28. Nxf7! wins a pawn, as recapturing with the rook loses to 29. Rd8+ and Qxc6. An alternative less convincing line was 28. Rxd7 Qxd7 29. Qa8+ Bf8 30. Nxh7! Kxh7 31. Qxf8, as queen endings are not always that easy to win.

Tal-Zeid, Soviet Union 1955

128

178) Black to play

47...h2+ 48. Kh1 Rb1+ 49. Kxh2 e2 50. b8Q e1Q 51. Qf8+ leads only to a perpetual. Winning is **47...Rb1+!** 48. Kh2 e2 49. Re3!(49. b8Q? Rh1+! 50. Kxh1 e1Q+ 51. Kh2 Qf2+ with mate on the next move, 52. Kh1 Qg2# or 52. Kxh3 Qg3#) fxe3 50. b8Q Rh1+ 51. Kxh1 e1Q+ 52. Kh2 Qf2+ 53. Kxh3 Qxf3+, followed by 54...e2, and the e2-passer wins the game for black.

Gipslis-Tal, Vilnius 1955

179) Black to play

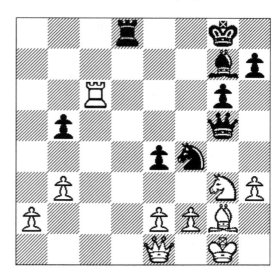

White threatens to consolidate with 31. e3. Therefore, black plays **30...e3!**, a nice and powerful break, winning in force. White is helpless:
a) 31. fxe3 Nxg2! 32. Kxg2 Qd5+, forking king and rook, using the fact the advance of the e-pawn has opened the h1-a8 diagonal
b) 31. f3 h5, followed by h4
c) 31. Rc1 exf2+ 32. Kxf2 Bd4+ 33. Kf1 Nxe2!

Klasup-Tal, Vilnius 1955

180) White to play

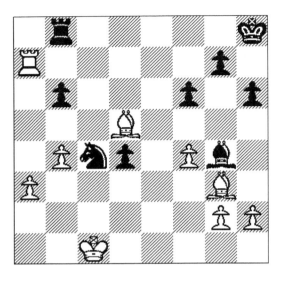

33.Bxc4? is now a mistake, which leads to fully equal after 33...Rc8 34. Kd2 Rxc4. The correct move is **33. f5!** Ne5/Rc8 34. Be6 and white, who has the bishop pair and more active pieces, should win.

Tal-Kliavins, Vilnius 1955

181) Black to play

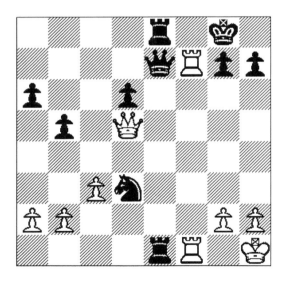

33...Qxf7! 34. Qxf7+ Kh8 35. Kg1 Rxf1+ 36. Qxf1 Re1 leaves black with

a piece more. 33...Qe6 is equivalent, but not that attractive. On the other hand, 33...Rxf1+ 34. Rxf1+ Qe6 35. Qxd3 gives fully equal, while 33...Qe2?? even loses to 34. Rf8#

Khasin-Tal, Leningrad 1956

182) Black to play

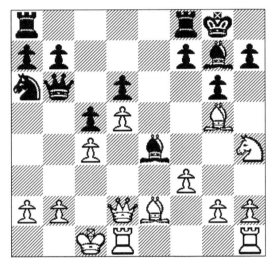

14...Nb4! wins:
a) 15. b3 Qa5
b) 15. fxe4 Nxa2+ 16. Kb1 Nc3+ 17. Kc1 Ne4! 18. Qc2(otherwise black mates on b2) Nxg5, leaving black 2 pawns up with the white king even more exposed

Chukaev-Tal, Tbilisi 1956

183) White to play

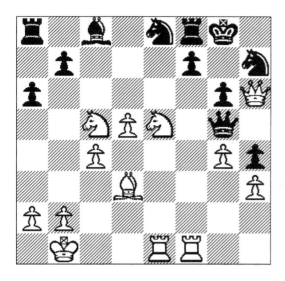

25. Nxf7! seals it:
a) 25...Rxf7? 26. Rxe8+ Rf8 27.
Rexf8+ Nxf8 28. Rxf8#
b) 25...Qxh6 26. Nxh6+ Kg7 27. Re7+
Kxh6 28. Rxh7+ Kxh7 29. Rxf8
25. Qxg5 also wins, but less
convincingly.

Tal-Georgadze, Tbilisi 1956

184) Black to play

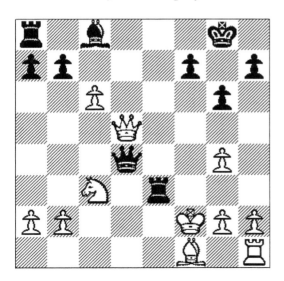

Tal played here the winning
17...Re2++ double check 18. Kxe2
Bxg4+ 19. Ke1 Re8+ 20. Be2
Rxe2+!(Nxe2 Qxd5). Different other
moves are also winning, for example
17...Qf4+ 18. Kg1 Rxc3!, threatening
Qe3 mate, or even 17...Rf3++ 18. Kxf3
Bxg4+ 19. Kg3 Qe3+! 20. Kxg4 h5+.
But not 17...Rxc3+?? 18. Qxd4.

Szukszta-Tal, Uppsala 1956

185) Black to play

33...Rxf4! 34. exf4 Qxd6 leaves black
with 2 connected passed pawns and an
easy win. Alternative moves, like
33...c4? give black excellent
counterplay after 34. Qe4!, followed by
Qe7, and the d-passer becomes very
strong, with d6-d7 already threatening.

Romani-Tal, Italy 1957

186) White to play

34. Qd6!(there are other winning
moves, but this is the most effective)
seals it:

a) 34...Rxd6 35. Rf8+ and Rh8#

b) 34...Rc8/Qc8 35. Ne7+ and then
Nxc8

c) 34...Re8/Ra8 35. Rf8+! Kh7 36.
Rxe8/a8

d) 34...Nc6/Ne6 35. Qxd8+! Nxd8 36.
Rf8+ and Rh8#

e) 34...Qd1+ 35. Rxd1 Rxd6 36. Rxd4

Tal-Scafarelli, Italy 1957

187) White to play

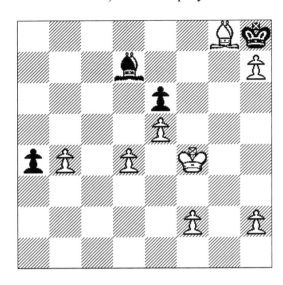

Black threatens to quickly promote the
a-pawn. 45. b5? a3 46. b6 a2 47. b7
a1Q 48. b8Q Qc1+ 49. Kf3 Qd1+ 50.
Kg3 Qg1+ is a perpetual. That is why,
45. d5! a3 46. dxe6 a2 47. exd7 a1Q
48. d8Q and white wins.

Tal-Petrosian, Moscow 1957

188) White to play

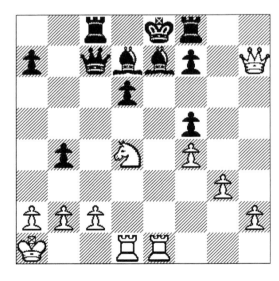

On 24. Qh4, black has 24...Be6! 25.
Nxe6 fxe6 26. Rxe6 Rf7 and black

might be even better. Therefore, the more energetic **24. Rxe7+!** is called for. After 24...Kxe7 25. Re1+ Kd8(Be6? Rxe6+!, the f7-pawn is pinned) 26. Qh4+ f6 27. Qh6!, attacking the rook on f8, and now:

a) 27...Rg8?? 28. Qxf6#

b) 27...Rf7 28. Qh8+, mating

c) 27...Qa5! resists for a while, but black is lost after 28. Nb3! Qd5 29. Qxf8+ Kc7 30. Qxf6; in above line, 28. Qxf8+? instead of Nb3 would be a blunder, as after 28...Kc7 29. Qxf6 black has 29...b3!, simultaneously attacking the rook on e1 and threatening mate on a2, and already black is on top.

Tal-Klaman, Moscow 1957

190) Black to play

189) Black to play

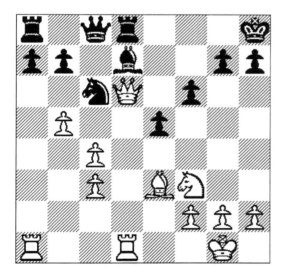

19...Bh3!, a discovered attack that wins:

a) 20. Qa3? Rxd1+ 21. Rxd1 Qg4, and after the knight retreats to e1 to defend mate, the d1-rook becomes an easy prey

b) 20. gxh3 Rxd6 21. Rxd6 Ne7 is hopeless

c) best is 20. bxc6 Rxd6 21. Rxd6, but after 21...Bg4 the outcome is clear

Taimanov-Tal, Moscow 1957

190) Black to play

29...Rd1? 30. Qxf6 Rxe1+ 31. Kh2 Qh6(Kf8 Qd6+ and Qxb8+) 32. Bxe1 wins for white.

The elegant correct move is **29...Bxc3!**, temporary queen sacrifice, 30. Rxc1 Bd4!, pinning the queen to the king, winning the exchange.

Bannik-Tal, Moscow 1957

191) Black to play

Other moves also win, but the most elegant solution is **55...Rxc1!** After 56. Rxc1(56. Rxe2 leads to an easily won rook ending) Bd1!, trapping the rook, black wins easily, for example 57. Kd2 Kg6 58. Ra1 Kxg5 59. Ra2 h5.

Benko-Tal, Reykjavik 1957

192) Black to play

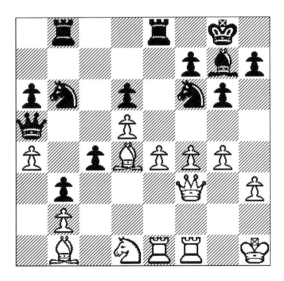

30...Nbxd5! wins a pawn(exd5? Rxe1), but not certainly the game, as white has the bishop pair. The alternative capture, 30...Nfxd5, looks weaker, as, after trade of dark-square bishops, the black king is vulnerable.

Mititelu-Tal, Reykjavik 1957

193) Black to play

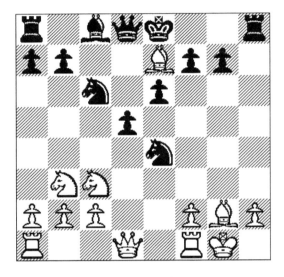

13...Qc7!, threatening mate on h2, gains a tempo. After 14. h3 Nxc3 15. bxc3(15. Bd8 or 15. Bd6 are slightly better, but those are purely engine tricks) Nxe7 white is hopeless.

Rannanjarvi-Tal, Reykjavik 1957

194) White to play

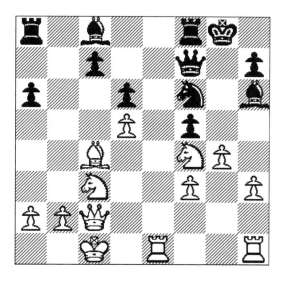

20. g5! wins material, for example, 20...Bxg5 21. Reg1 Qg7 22. Kb1 Bxf4(h3-h4 threatens) 23. Rxg7+ Kxg7 24. Ne2 Alternatives lead to similar developments.

Tal-Dittmann, Reykjavik 1957

195) Black to play

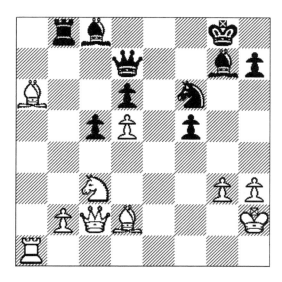

29...Qa7! wins:
a) 30. Bxc8 Qxa1 31. Be6+ Kh8 leaves black the exchange up

b) 30. Qd3 Rxb2 is weaker
c) in case of 30. Qa4 Bxa6 31. Qxa6 Qxa6 32. Rxa6 Rxb2 33. Ra2 Rxa2 34. Nxa2 Nxd5 wins

Skuja-Tal, Latvia 1958

196) White to play

25. Ne7+! Kh8 26. Qxe5+ f6 27. Qxf6+! Rxf6 28. Rxd8+ mates. 25. Nf6+ also wins. Bur not 25. Qxe5?? Qxc2#.

Tal-Skuja, Latvia 1958

197) Black to play

9...Qe3+ wins a pawn:
a) 10. Qe2 Qxf4
b) 10. Be2 Nxe4 11. Nxe4 Qxf4!,
attacking both the knight on e4 and
bishop on h4, 12. Nxd6+ Bxd6;
Stockfish gives 11...Qxe4 12. 0-0 as
better for white, though, as the black
queen is exposed to attacks from the
white army, which will gain some
tempos

Fichtl-Tal, Munich 1958

198) Black to play

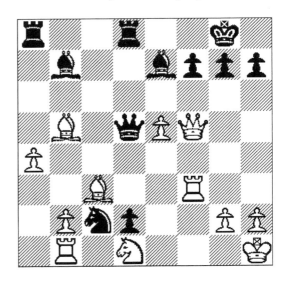

32...Ne1! and black wins:
a) 33. Rg3/f2 Nxg2
b) 33. Ne3 Qxf3! 34. gxf3 Nxf3 35.
Qf4 Ng5+! 36. Kg1 Nh3+, forking
queen and king

Beni-Tal, Munich 1958

199) White to play

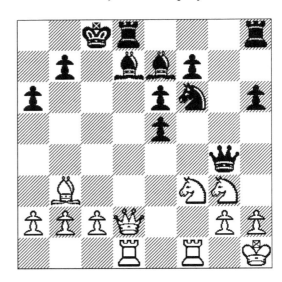

22. Nxe5 Qg8(other retreats are even
worse) 23. Nh5 and white wins:

136

a) 23...Nxh5 24. Nxd7
b) 23...Bb5 24. Qc3+ Kb8 25. Rxd8+
Qxd8 26. Nxf7
22...Bc6 23. Nxg4 Rxd2 24. Rxd2
Nxg4 25. Rxf7 is similarly hopeless.

Tal-Larsen, Portoroz 1958

200) White to play

The white bishop on d2 is under attack.
If 28. Qxe5??, then 28...Rxd2. If the
bishop retreats, for example 28. Rc1?,
then 28...Rxd1 29. Rxd1 Rxd1 30.
Bxd1 31. Nxe4!, followed by Nxf2+
28. Be3 is similar. Therefore, **28.
Bxh6!** is called for, it is true that after
28...gxh6(28...Rxd1?? 29. Bxg7+) 29.
Qxe5 Be7 30. Rd4 white might not be
winning in the complications, but at
least he will not lose.

Tal-Filip, Portoroz 1958

201) White to play

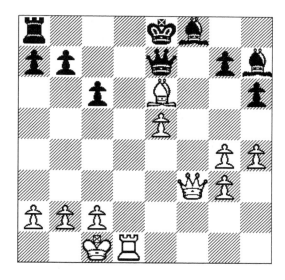

22. Bd7+ Qxd7 23. Rxd7 Kxd7 24.
Qf7+ Be7 25. e6+ Kd6 26. Qxg7 wins
too much material.

Tal-Fuster, Portoroz 1958

202) White to play

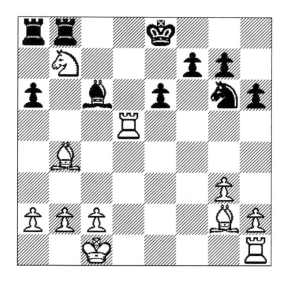

24. Rd8+! Rxd8 25. Bc6+ Rd7 26.
Nd6+ is more than convincing. 24.
Nd6+ Kd7 25. Rd2 Bxg2 26. Nxf7+
also wins, while much weaker.

137

Tal-Kliavins, Riga 1958

203) Black to play

18...Ng4! 19. hxg4 Bxc3 20. Rc1 Bg7 leaves black better(the g-pawns are doubled). Alternatives are weaker, for example 18...Nd4 19. bxc5 dxc5 20. Nd5 with some white edge.

Kotov-Tal, Riga 1958

204) Black to play

Here the simple **33...gxf4** 34. fxg4 Qxg4 was winning. Tal blundered with 33...Nf2?, where 34. Qb3+, an intermediate check, 34...Kg7 35. Be3 Nh3 36. Bxd4 cxd4 37. Qd5 gives already white some advantage.

Kotov-Tal, Riga 1958

205) Black to play

Different moves win for black here, but the one played by Tal, **47...Re1!!**, is most effective and leads to the quickest win. The c2-pawn threatens to promote at any moment, for example 48. Rxe1 Rd1.

Kotov-Tal, Riga 1958

206) White to play

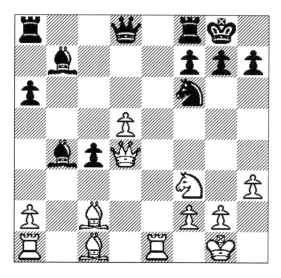

The position is fully equal and Tal should have accepted the draw with **18. Rd1** Qxd5 19. Rb1, leading to big simplifications. Instead he played 18. Rb1?, which Stockfish shows as giving definite advantage for black after 18...Bxe1 19. Rxb7 Ba5 20. d6 Rb8, with which I fully agree.

Tal-Geller, Riga 1958

207) White to play

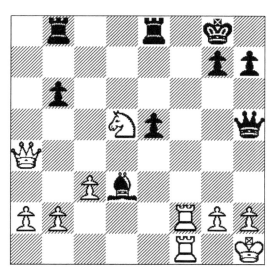

Here Tal played 29. g4?, which Stockfish shows as losing after 29...Qh4(attacking the f2-rook, so that the rook on f1 can not retreat) 30. Ne3 Bxf1 31. Rxf1 Rf8. Alternatives should draw, as, although white is a pawn up, the black central passer is very dangerous.

Tal-Furman, Riga 1958

208) Black to play

70...Rh1+ and now:
a) 71. Rh2 Rxh2+ 72. Kxh2 Qe2+ 73. Kh3 Qf1+ 74. Kh2 Kg4! and white can not defend(Qh3+ and Qxg3+ threatens, for example)
b) 71. Kg2 Qe4+ 72. Rf3 Kg4 73. Qc8+ f5 74. Qc3 Rh3! ends the struggle, Rxg3+ threatens, on 75. Kf2 black has 75...Rh2+ and Qe2

Spassky-Tal, Riga 1958

209) Black to play

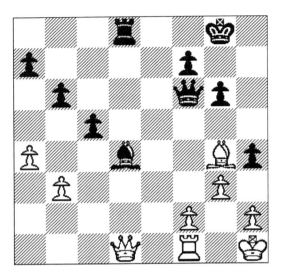

30...Bxf2! 31. Qf3 Qxf3 32. Bxf3 hxg3 wins at least a pawn. 31. Qe2 is weaker because of 31...Rd2! and white can not take the rook due to 32...Qc6+ 33. Bf3 Qxf3#.

Averbakh-Tal, Riga 1958

210) Black to play

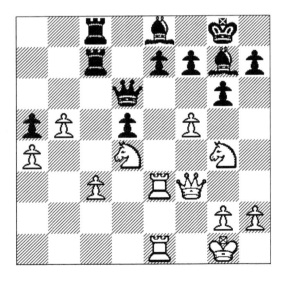

26...Rxc3! and now:

a) 27. Rxc3 Bxd4+ 28. Rce3 Rc3 is very convincing
b) 27. f6 is a good attempt, but after 27...Rxe3 28. Qxe3 Bxf6 29. Nxf6+ exf6 the outcome makes no doubt

Gurgenidze-Tal, Riga 1958

211) Black to play

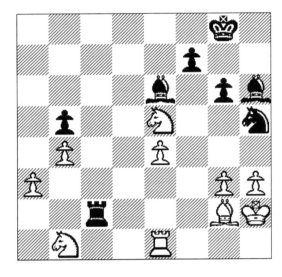

Although white is 2 pawns up, the black bishops dominate the board, while the b1-knight is trapped.
33...Nf4!, very elegant solution, and now:
a) 34. gxf4 Bxf4+ 35. Kh1 Bxe5 is hopeless for white, black will later pick more material
b) 34. Rg1 Nxh3! is also convincing in a similar vein

Klasup-Tal, Soviet Union 1958

212) White to play

There might be other winning moves, but **13. e6!**, opening the black king position, is strongest, with a certain demise.

Tal-Kampenus, Soviet Union 1958

213) White to play

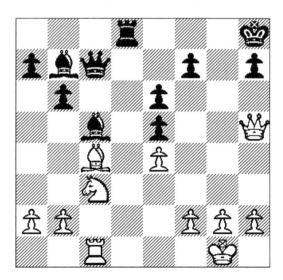

Black has the bishop pair, so white must be very careful. 19. Rd1 Rxd1+ 20. Qxd1 Qe7 will hardly fully equalise

or any other unambitious move, for that matter. Therefore, **19. Nb5!** Qe7(19...Qb8? 20. b4!, followed by Qxf7, is decisive) 20. Qxe5+ f6 21. Qf4 e5 22. Qg4, and Stockfish now gives this line fully equal after 22...Bxf2+ 23. Kxf2 Qxc5+ and Qxc4.

Tal-Portisch, Varna 1958

214) White to play

24. Rxe5+!! is both effective and efficient:
a) 24...dxe5 25. d6+ Ke8 26. d7+ Kd8 27. Qd6 will mate shortly
b) 24...fxe5 25. Qg5+ Ke8 26. Qf6 with the double threat of taking on h8 and d6, followed by a deadly check on d7. If 25...Kf8 26. Qf6 Kg8, then 27. Be6! fxe6 28. Rf1 decides in an elegant and surprising way.

Tal-Malich, Varna 1958

141

215) White to play

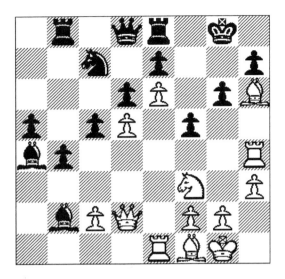

The logical **23. Bf8!**, clearing squares and files for the heavy pieces, leads to a forced mate:
a) 23...Kxf8 24. Rxh7 Bg7 25. Qg5!, followed by Qxg6
b) 23...Rxf8 24. Qh6 Rf7 25. Ng5!(exf7+ is also possible) Rg7 26. Nxh7

Tal-Benko, Bled 1959

216) Black to play

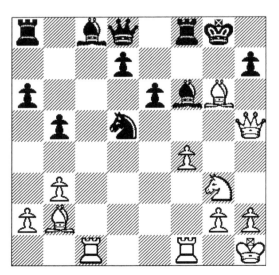

22...hxg6?? 23. Qxg6+ Kh8 24. Rf3!, aiming at h3, wins for white. After the correct **22...Qe7!**, defending h7, 23. Bxf6 Nxf6 24. Qf3 Bb7 the game is more or less equal.

Olafsson-Tal, Bled 1959

217) Black to play

If the knight retreats, Qxf7+ and Qg8#. On 24...d3??, black has 25. gxf6+ Kf8 26. Qg3! Therefore, **24...Kf8!** and now:
a) 25. exf6? Qc3 wins for black, as, although attacking, the white minors are uncomfortably placed on the edge of the board, while the d3-passer very dangerous
b) 25. Bxf6 Qc1+ 26. Kh2 Qxh6 27. Bg5 Qg7 28. Bf6 Rxf6 29. exf6 Qh6 is an endgame, that has reached dynamic equality

218) White to play

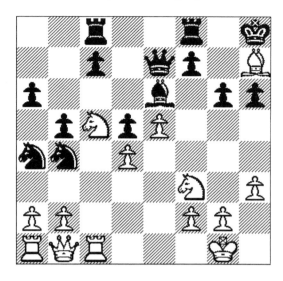

White has no better than **22. Bxg6**
Nxc5 23. Rxc5 fxg6 24. Qxg6 Bf5 25.
Qxh6+ Qh7 26. Qxh7 Bxh7 with
equality.

Tal-Olafsson, Bled 1959

219) White to play

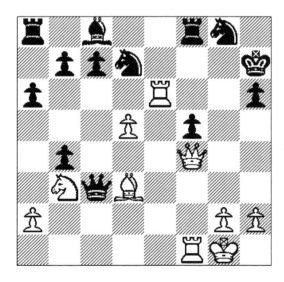

24. Bxf5+! decides:
a) 24...Rxf5 25. Qxf5+ Kh8 26. Rf3!
Qg7 27. Rg3, threatening Re8 pin

b) 24...Kg7(Kh8 Rxh6+) 25. Rg6+ Kf7
26. Bd3+ Ke7 27. Qe3+ Ne5 28. Rg7+,
and in the kingdom of pins, black can
not save himself

Tal-Fischer, Bled 1959

220) White to play

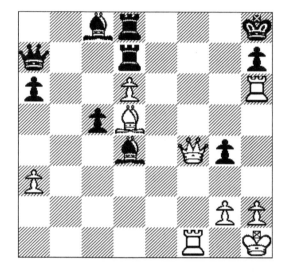

41. Rf6! decides:
a) 41...Bxf6 42. Qxf6+ Rxg7 43.
Qxd8+
b) 41...Rg7 42. Rf8+
c) 41...Rg8 42. Rf8

Tal-Smyslov, Bled 1959

143

221) White to play

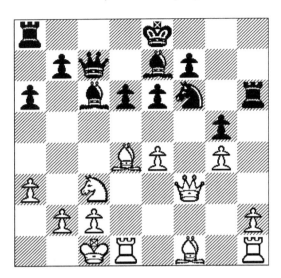

17. h4! is a very nice move:
a) 17...gxh4? 18. g5 forks rook and knight
b) 17...Rxh4? 18. Rxh4 gxh4 19. Bxf6 loses a piece
c) on other options, white threatens to create strong defended passer with h4-h5, or later open the h-file for active play
White certainly can not hope to get good play with alternative moves.

Tal-Olafsson, Bled 1959

222) White to play

40. e5! ends the game:
a) 40...Rf8 41. exd6 g5 42. Qe4+ Kg8 43. Qe6+ Kh7 44. Qe7+ Kg8 45. Qxf8+! Kxf8 46. Ng6++
b) 40...dxe5 41. Qd7+ Kg8 42. Qd8+ Kf7 43. Qxc7+ Kg8 44. Qd8+ Kf7 45. Qd7+ and c7

Tal-Fischer, Bled 1959

223) Black to play

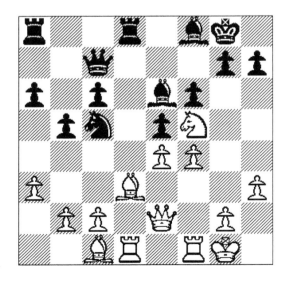

19...Bxf5! 20. exf5 e4 21. Bxe4 Re8 22. Rd4 Rad8 23. Rfd1(Rxd8 Qxd8) Rxd4 24. Rxd4 Qe7 and the e4-bshop falls.

Abrosimov-Tal, Riga 1959

224) Black to play

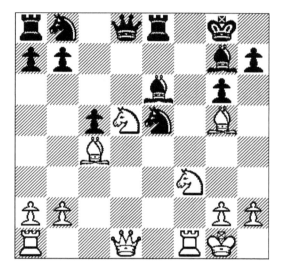

16...Nxf3+ 17. Qxf3 Qxg5 18. Rae1(18. Nc7? Bxc4 19. Nxe8 Bd4+ is hopeless) Nc6 19. Rxe6 Rf8 should be winning for black, who is left with a pawn more.

Niemela-Tal, Riga 1959

225) White to play

27. Qc6 also wins, but most convincing is **27. Qe8+!**(to make the black rook inactive) Rf8 28. Qc6 Rf6 29. Re3, intending Qf3.

Tal-Franz, Riga 1959

226) White to play

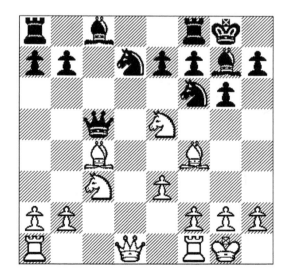

Here Tal played 12. Bxf7+?!, which Stockfish sees as favouring black after 12...Rxf7 13. Nxf7 Kxf7 14. Qb3+ Kf8,

and then offering exchange of queens
on b6. **12. Qd4** is fully equal.

Tal-Johannessen, Riga 1959

227) White to play

21. Rc6! Qf7 22. Nc7 wins. All the
variations are not possible to see, but
white gets very active. In above line
black can not play 21...Qxc6??, as 22.
Qxe7+ Kg8 23. Qxe8+ Bf8 24. Ne7+
loses the queen.

Tal-Johannessen, Riga 1959

228) White to play

26. Nxa5! and now:
a) 26...Qd7 27. Nc6 Rb7 28. Rfd1 is
very convincing
b) 26...Bxf1 27. Nc6 Qd7 28. Nxb4
Ba6 29. Nxa6 Nxa6 30. Qc4 even more
so

Tal-Pietzsch, Riga 1959

229) White to play

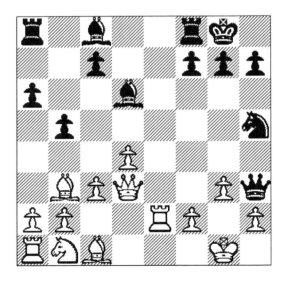

16. Bd5!, a typical manoeuvre in the Marshall Gambit, after 16...Bf5 17. Qe3 Rad8 18. Bg2!, the bishop comes to guard the friendly king with tempo, and white has very nice position.

Tal-Witkowski, Riga 1959

230) Black to play

26...Nxe5! wins another pawn:
a) 27. fxe5 Rxc5
b) 27. Nxb7 Nxd3 28. cxd3 Kxf6
c) 27. Nh5+ gxh5 28. Nxb7 Nxd3 29. cxd3 Rc7

Tolush-Tal, Riga 1959

231) White to play

32. Ra3!, this is winning, as well as the only good way to avoid Rh1+ and Rxa1. The rook stays behind the friendly passed pawn. On 32. Rc1? or 32. Rd1?, after black makes a luft with g7-g5, his rook will take position behind the enemy passed pawns on b2 or a2 and white can only hope for a draw. Now, the march of the a-passer is forceful.

Tal-Averbakh, Tbilisi 1959

232) White to play

49. Ne8! is best, easily deciding. This is a very trappy position. In order to win, white should avoid at least the following moves:
a) 49. Rxc7? Rxd6+ and Ra6 with draw
b) 49. Nc4? Rb7 50. Rxc7 Rxc7 51. a8Q Rxc4 with a fortress position
c) 49. Nf7? Rb2+! 50. Kd3 Rb3+ 51. Ke4 Rb4+ with perpetual check. If the white king goes to f5, then Rf4 mates, while if he crosses the c-file, Rb7! even wins for black, as, when white takes the knight on c7, black retakes with check and later also the a-passer.

Tal-Averbakh, Tbilisi 1959

233) Black to play

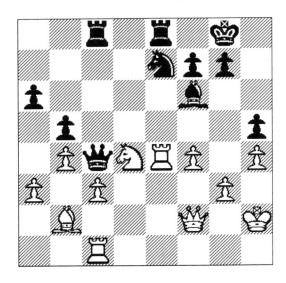

28...Nf5 is best, winning tempo to transfer the knight via h6 to g4, bearing in mind that 29. Rxe8+ Rxe8 30. Nxf5?? is impossible, because of 30...Re2.

Vasiukov-Tal, Tbilisi 1959

234) White to play

29. Rd5! Bxd5 30. Rxd5 Rf6 31. Bxf5 gives white sufficient positional

148

advantage, as the e4-pawn is weak and will fall at some point too.

Tal-Gurgenidze, Tbilisi 1959

236) Black to play

235) Black to play

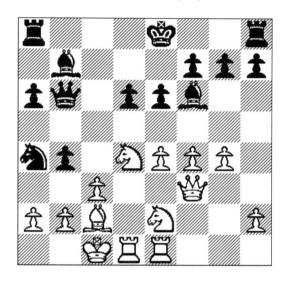

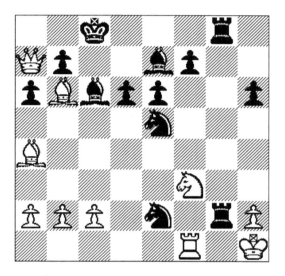

16...Nxb2! 17. Kxb2 bxc3++ 18. Kxc3 Rc8+ 19. Kd3 0-0! leaves the white king permanently in the center, promising black good winning chances. Alternatives(the a4-knight is under attack) are not good.

Jupper-Tal, Zurich 1959

25...Rg1+! 26. Bxg1 Bxf3+ 27. Rxf3 Rxg1+ 28. Qxg1 Nxg1 29. Rc3+ Kd8 30. Kxg1 d5 leaves black almost certainly winning. Huge blunder, on the other hand, is 25...Nxf3??, because of 26. Qa8+ Kd7 27. Qxb7+ with mate in 2.

Nikitin-Tal, Tbilisi 1959

237) Black to play

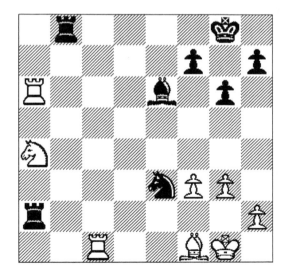

34...Nxf1 35. Kxf1(Rxf1 Bc4 is identical) Bc4+! is a nice finish,

149

subsequently capturing the rook on a6. Taking the checking bishop is impossible, because of Rb1+, leading to a back rank mate.

Blau-Tal, Zurich 1959

239) Black to play

238) White to play

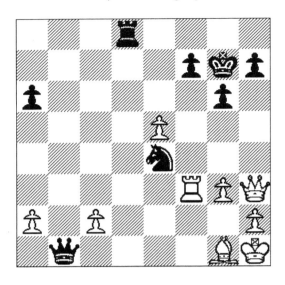

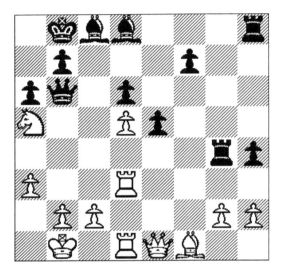

The knight is attacked and white should decide what to do with it. 24. b4? exposes too much the king, while 24. Nb3 Bf5 is quite good for black, who has the bishop pair. Therefore, **24. Nc6**+ Ka8(Bxc6?? Rb3) 25. Rb3 Qc7 26. Rc3 Qd7 27. Nxd8 Qxd8 28. Qf2 and white has some chances to defend successfully.

Tal-Nievergelt, Zurich 1959

30...Qb7! is the right move, easily winning after 31. Qg2 Rd2 32. Rb3 Nxg3+ 33. Rxg3 Rxg2 34. Rxg2 Qe4. 30...Nd2? 31. Rf4 is almost equal, while 30...Rd1? is met by the surprising 31. Rxf7+! Kxf7 32. Qxh7+ Ke6 33. Qxg6+ Kd5 34. Qf7+ Kc6 35. Qe8+ with a perpetual.

Walther-Tal, Zurich 1959

240) White to play

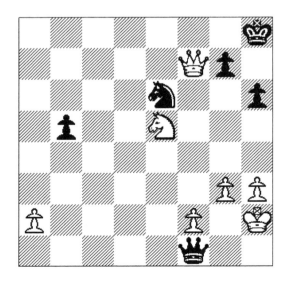

150

38. Ng6+! Kh7 39. Ne7 Qxh3+! 40. Kg1(Kxh3? Ng5+ and Nxf7 is draw) h5 41. Qg6+ Kh8 42. Nf5 ends the struggle. A range of alternatives might not win. For example, on 38. Nd7 38...Ng5 is good, while 38. Ng4 Qxh3+ 39. Kxh3 Ng5+ and Nxf7 is a straightforward draw. 38. Qxe6? Qxf2+ 39. Kh1 Qh1+ 40. Kh2 Qf2+ is a perpetual, of course.

Tal-Lehmann, Hamburg 1960

241) Black to play

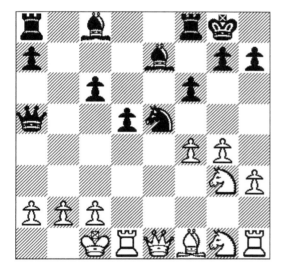

16...Qxa2! 17. fxe5 fxe5! and white is hopeless, Bg5+ threatens. 17...Qa1+ and Qxb2 is an alternative.

Troger-Tal, Hamburg 1960

242) Black to play

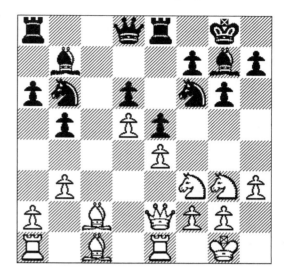

19...Nfxd5!, a clearance sacrifice, 20. exd5 e4 and now:
a) 21. Nxe4 Bxa1 22. Bg5 f6 23. Qd1 fxg5 24. Qxa1 Rf8 25. Nexg5 Bd5 and black has good winning chances
b) 21. Rb1? exf3 22. Qxe8+ Qxe8 23. Rxe8+ Rxe8 24. gxf3 Nxd5 is even worse

Unzicker-Tal, Hamburg 1960

243) White to play

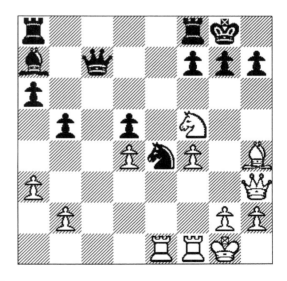

21. Rxe4!, removing the guard of the f6-square, 21...dxe4 22. Bf6, followed by Bxg7, decides.

Tal-Najdorf, Leipzig 1960

245) White to play

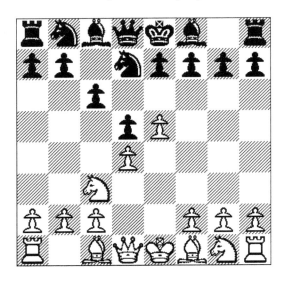

244) White to play

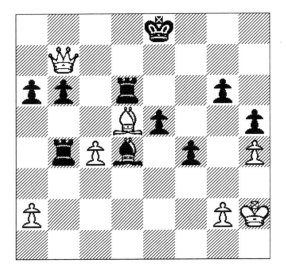

5. e6! fxe6 6. Nf3 Qc7 7. Qe2!, keeping the bind on e5, ensures white big development advantage, as black can not counter in the center.

Tal-Campomanes, Leipzig 1960

Other moves might also be winning, but most straightforward is **39. Bc6+** Rxc6 40. Qxc6+ Ke7 41. Qxg6 Rb2 42. Qxh5. If 39...Kf8, 40. Qb8+ Ke7 41. Qe8+ Kf6 42. Bd5

Tal-Ghitescu, Leipzig 1960

Advanced Tal

246) White to play

247) Black to play

22. Rxg7!! Absolutely brilliant. This was played as Tal was just starting his career. All lines lead to a forced mate:
a) 22...Kxg7 23. Rg1+ Kf8 24. Qg3 and Qg7
b) 22...Kxg7 23. Rg1+ Kh6 24. Qf4+ Kxh5 25. Qf3+ with mate to follow
c) 22...fxe5 23. Rf7+ Ke8 24. Rxe7++ Kf8 25. Rf1+ Kg8 26. Nf6+ Kf8 27. Rf7#

Tal-Gulko, Exhibition 1949

31...c6! 32. Rd2 Rxh3! wins here. Tal missed that one and instead played 31...g4?, which would allow white to deliver a perpetual, 32. Rxe5+! dxe5 33. Rd5!! gxh3 34. Qxe5+, as Stockfish shows. 33...Rxd5 34. cxd5+ Kd7 35. Qc6+ Kc8 36. Qa8+ Kd7 37. Qd5+ is also a perpetual. Very surprising, even for Tal.

Leonov-Tal, Soviet Union 1950

248) Black to play

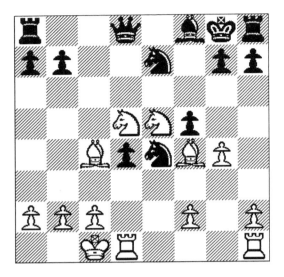

14...Qxd5! is the right move, which after 15. Rxd4 Qxc4 leaves black with a minor piece more. 14...Nxd5? instead is weaker, as after 15. Rxd4 Nef6 16. g5! white regains a large quantity of material, while keeping his pieces active.

Gutnikov-Tal, Leningrad 1951

249) Black to play

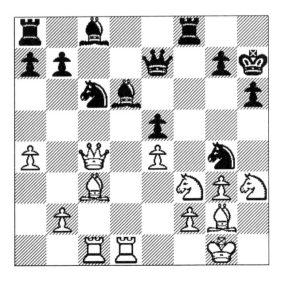

Here Tal played 20...Ne3?!, which proves to be a mistake, as white could have gotten the upper hand after 21. fxe3 Bxh3 22. Bxh3 Rxf3 23. Bf5+!(important intermediate move) g6 24. Kg2 Rxe3 25. Rxd6!, deflecting the queen from guarding the f7-square, as Stockfish shows. Tal's opponent played 21. Nhg5+?
Instead of the move in the game, black is better after 20...Bc5 or 20...a5, for example.

Ragozin-Tal, Riga 1951

250) Black to play

27...Nd4! 28. exd4 Rxd4(threatening deadly discovered check after for example Qa2 Rxd2+) 29. Kg2 Rxc4 and black won. White could have defended better with 28. Kg2! Nxf3(28...Nxc2 is a huge blunder, as white mates after 29. Rh1+ Kg6 30. Bh5+ Kf6 31. Rf1#) 29. Rxf3 Rxf3 30. Kxf3, although after 30...g4+! black is still on top.

Tal missed the more convincing
27...Rxd2! 28. Rxd2 Bxe3+ though(29.
Rdf2 Rxf3).

Ragozin-Tal, Riga 1951

251) Black to play

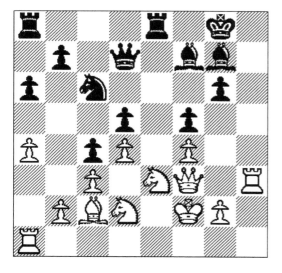

27...Nxd4! 28. cxd4 Bxd4 creates a
deadly absolute pin plus 2 strong
central pawns in terms of
compensation, quite probably sufficient
for a win. The concrete lines are very
long to show, but black always has the
advantage. The important thing is to
realise the power of such pins.

Klevetzki-Tal, Riga 1952

252) White to play

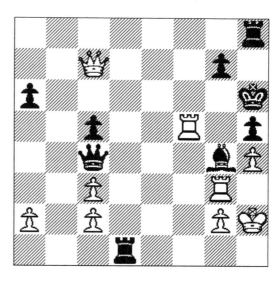

Here Tal played 39. Rxh5+?(39...Bxh5
40. Qxg7#), which loses after
39...Kxh5 40. Qxg7 Qg8! 41. Qe5+
Kxh4, according to Stockfish. White
had a win with **39. Qe7!!** instead, for
example 39...g6 40. Rf7!(threatening
deadly checks on e3 and g5) Qxf7 41.
Qxf7.

Tal-Klasup, Riga 1952

253) Black to play

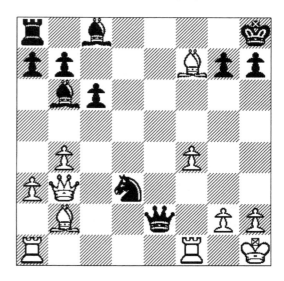

155

24...Bh3!!, the 2 exclamation marks are for effectiveness, and white is defenceless:
a) 25. gxh3 Qe4+ mates
b) 25. Rg1(the g2-square is attacked) Nf2# too
c) only way to defend is to sacrifice material after 25. Bxg7+ Kxg7 26. Bd5(protecting g2) cxd5 27. Qxd5, but 27...Rg8! 28. gxh3 Kh8 29. Qf3 Rg1+! is still a nice finish
Black could also have blundered with 24...Nxb2?? 25. Rae1 and suddenly the roles change due to the mate threat on e8.

Klasup-Tal, Soviet Union 1952

254) Black to play

17...Ng3+!, obvious move, but very elegant. All lines lose by force:
a) capturing with the knight or bishop leads to the double threat of mate on h2 and winning the loose queen on d2, for example 18. Nxg3 fxg3 19. Be3(Bxg3 Qxd2) Qxe3! 20. Qxe3 Rxh2#
b) 18. Rxg3 loses in a splendid way after 18...Rxh2+!(subtle intermediate move) 19. Kg1(Kxh2 fxg3+ and Qxd2) Qh6!(building a battery and threatening Rh1+ and Qh2#) 20. Kf1(only defence) Rxf2+!(kind of a strange windmill) 21. Ke1(21. Kxf2 fxg3+ 22. Ke1 Qh1+! 23. Ng1 Qxg1+) fxg3 and black is a whole rook up
c) best is 18. Kg2! Qh4! 19. Bxg3 fxg3 20. hxg3 Qh2+ 21. Kf1 Rf6, with black winning material and still being on the attack

Pasman-Tal, Soviet Union 1952

255) White to play

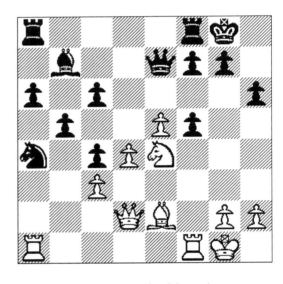

19. Nf6+! and white wins:
a) 19...gxf6 20. Qxh6 fxe5 21. Rf3!(third rank lift that decides) f4(Rg3+ has been threatening) 22. Rh3 f6 23. Qh8+ Kf7 24. Rh7+ Ke8 25. Rxe7+ Kxe7 26. Qg7+ and the black king is too exposed
b) 19...Kh8 fails to 20. Rxf5 Rfd8 21. Rh5!(a sacrifice on h6 is imminent) Qf8 22. Rf1, followed by Rf4-h4 and the h6-point falls

Tal-Zeid, Soviet Union 1952

156

256) Black to play

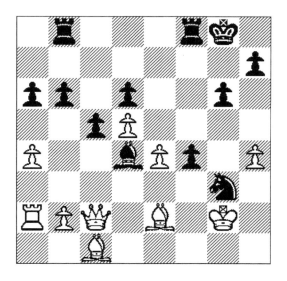

Taking with the knight or bishop on c8 will allow white to capture the queen on d2 and then occupy the open file with Rc1 first, which will most probably lead to a draw. Black has much stronger with **21...Ke7!**, though. After 22. Rxh8 Qxa2 23. Nbd2 Qc2!(protecting the h7 pawn), he enjoys big advantage. It is true that the pair of rooks are stronger than the queen, but the white knights are redundant and especially the black rook on the 8th rank is more offside and vulnerable than attacker.

Listengarten-Tal, Kharkov 1953

33...Nxe2 wins:
a) 34. Qxe2 f3+, forking queen and king, 35. Qxf3 Rxf3 36. Kxf3 Rf8+
b) 34. Ra3 Nxc1 35. Qxc1 b5 and black has many pieces and passers, while still being on the attack

Birbrager-Tal, Kharkov 1953

257) Black to play

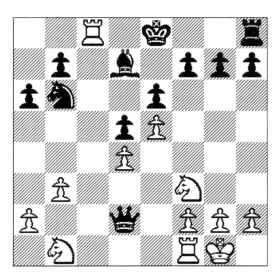

258) Black to play

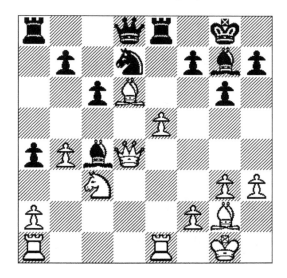

18...Nxe5!, defending the c4-bishop and threatening Nf3+ is very convincing:
a) 19. Bxe5 Qxd4 20. Bxd4 Bxd4
b) 19. Rxe5 Rxe5!(but not 19...Bxe5? 20. Bxe5 and already white is on top) 20. Qxc4 Qxd6

Gradus-Tal, Soviet Union 1953

259) Black to play

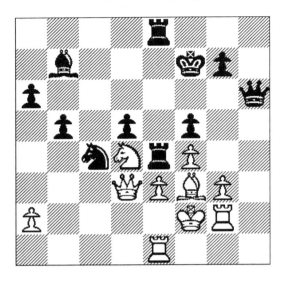

43...Nxe3! 44. Bxe4 Ng4+(an important intermediate move) 45. Kg1 fxe4 46. Qe2 Qh5 easily wins, black threatens Rh8. 43...Rxe3 is just a draw after 44. Qxf5+ Kg8 45. Rxe3 Nxe3 46. Qd7, according to Stockfish, but the lines are complicated.

Darznieks-Tal, Latvia 1954

260) White to play

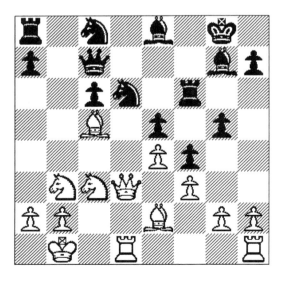

Here Tal played 21. Nd5?!, which after 21...cxd5 22. Qxd5+ Nf7 23. Qxa8 Bc6 24. Bb6!(untrapping the queen) axb6 25. Rc1!, pinning in turn the c6-bishop, Bf8 26. Bb5 Bxa8 27. Rc7 Ncd6 leads only to draw, with black even being a tiny bit better, according to Stockfish, whose opinion I share too. Instead, alternative moves like 21. h4 or 21. Bf2 retain clear edge for white. Maybe one of the cases, where Tal should not have sacrificed.

Tal-Visockiss, Riga 1954

261) Black to play

Here Tal played **25...Ne3!** Other moves also win, but this is effective. After 26. fxe3 Bxe3+ 27. Kh1 Bxd2 28. Qxd2 Re2 white is hopeless. Of course, not 25...fxg5??, because of 26. Qxg7 mate.

Saigin-Tal, Riga 1954

158

262) White to play

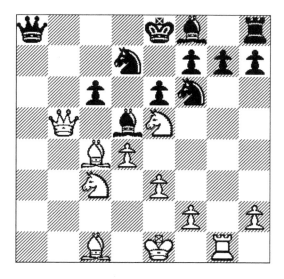

16. Bxd5! Nxe5 17. Bh1! cxb5 18. Bxa8 Bb4 19. dxe5 Bxc3+ 20. Bd2 Bxe5 leads to fully equal. If the queen retreats or after 16. Nxd5 exd5 black stays with a pawn more.

Tal-Akmentin, Soviet Union 1954

263) Black to play

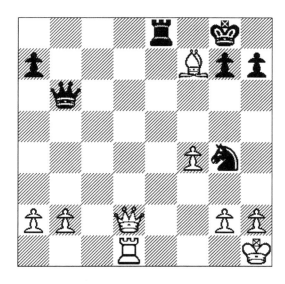

25...Kf8! 26. Bxe8 Nf2+ 27. Kg1 Nxd1+ 28. Kf1 Ne3+ 29. Ke2 Nc4!(an

important intermediate move, threatening the queen) 30. Qd3 Qe6+!(defending the knight) 31. Kf2 Kxe8 32. b3 Nd6 33. Qxh7 leads to black advantage in a knight for 3 pawns endgame. 25...Kxf7? instead cedes the edge to white after 26. Qd7+ and Qxg4.

Arulaid-Tal, Lugansk 1955

264) Black to play

18...Rxf3! gives black considerable advantage:
a) 19. gxf3 Nxd4!, with Nxe2+ and Nxf3+, followed by Nxg5, threatening
b) 19. hxg4 Nxd4, with similar motifs

Rovner-Tal, Riga 1955

265) White to play

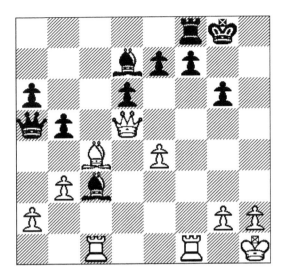

24. Rxf7! bxc4 25. Rcf1 is easily winning for white:
a) 25...Rxf7? 26. Qxf7+ Kh8 27. Qf8+ Kh7 28. Rf7+ Bg7 29. Qxg7#
b) 25...Qxd5 26. Rxf8+ Kh7 27. exd5
c) 25...Re8 26. Rf8+ Kh7 27. Qg8+ Kh6 28. Rxe8 Bxe8 29. Qxe8 and white has no problems converting

Tal-Vasiukov, Riga 1955

266) White to play

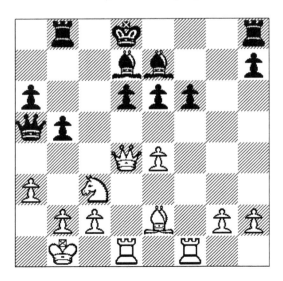

20. Rxf6! wins a pawn. Black will have to trade queens with 20...Qb6, otherwise white crashes in:
a) 20...Bxf6? 21. Qxf6+ Kc7(otherwise white captures the h8-rook with check) 22. e5! d5 23. Nxd5! exd5 24. Qd6+ Kc8 25. Rxd5
b) 20...e5? 21. Qf2 and the d5-square is weak; if 21...b4, then 22. Rfxd6! is decisive
c) on 20...b4 different moves, among which 21. Rf5 and 21. Rxe6, win

Tal-Furman, Riga 1955

267) White to play

16. dxe5! Rxd3 17. exf6 Bd6 18. Ne4 ensures white nice edge. Tal played 16. Qf3?!, unpinning the d4-pawn and winning f6, but Stockfish sees it as only equal after 16...Qc7 17. Qxf6 Rh6 18. Qf3 f5! Although without a pawn, black develops quite some initiative on the king side, placing the rooks on the g and h-files. Capturing the h5-pawn is dangerous. f5-f4 also threatens in a range of lines.

Tal-Goldin, Soviet Union 1955

268) White to play

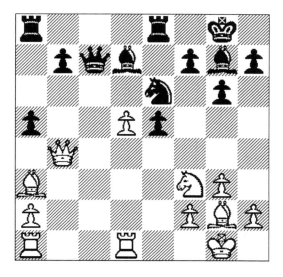

If white retreats the queen now, the simple Nd4 leaves black a pawn up. **20. dxe6!**, great move on the part of Tal, gives white some edge after 20...axb4 21. Rxd7 Qxd7! 22. exd7 Red8 23. Bxb4, although Stockfish sees the complications arising with 23...e4 as only leading to a draw. Retreating with the queen after 21. Rxd7 is a blunder, as white picks up too much material after 22. exf7+ and 23. fxe8Q+

Tal-Skuja, Soviet Union 1955

269) Black to play

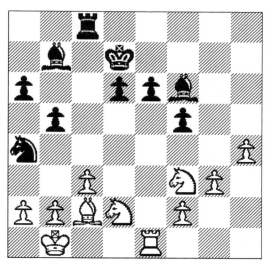

26...Nxb2! is a nice temporary sacrifice. After 27. Kxb2 Bxf3! 28. Nxf3 Rxc3 black threatens to recapture on f3 with check. If the knight moves, then 29...Re3+, followed by Rxe1, wins. On 29. Ne5+!?, 29...Bxe5 30. Rxe5 Rxc2+! 31. Kxc2 dxe5 leads to a winning pawn endgame. Tal however made a mistake with 27...Rxc3?, after which white had a draw with 28. Ne5+! Bxe5 29. Rxe5 Rxc2+ 30. Kxc2 dxe5 31. Nb3. The bishop versus knight endgame, in distinction to the plain pawn endgame, is not won for black due to the very active white knight.

Krimer-Tal, Vilnius 1955

270) White to play

If the knight retreats, black will be able to consolidate. Therefore, **12. Nxf7!** Kxf7 13. f5! and the exposed black king gives white more than sufficient compensation.

Tal-Simagin, Leningrad 1956

271) White to play

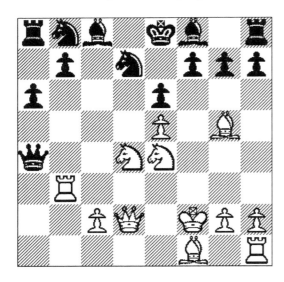

15. Nxe6! fxe6 16. Nd6+ Bxd6 17. Qxd6 wins for white. Tal, however,

played 15. Bb5?, which after 15...axb5 16. Nxb5 f6 might even lose for white.

Tal-Tolush, Leningrad 1956

272) White to play

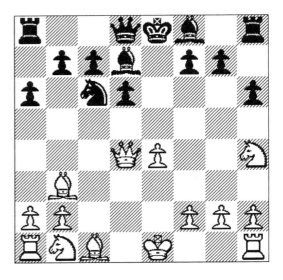

Here Tal played 11. Bxf7+?!, which, however, according to Stockfish, only leads to black advantage after 11...Kxf7 12. Qd5+ Be6 13. Qh5+ Kg8 14. Ng6 Qe8! 15. Nf4 Qxh5 16. Nxh5 Nb4, and black has the bishop pair, while being very active at the same time. The correct move, according to the engine, is **11. Qd5!**, which after 11...Qxh4 12. Qxf7+ Kd8 13. Nc3 gives white the edge. One should trust top engines in such highly tactical positions.

Tal-Bannik, Leningrad 1956

273) White to play

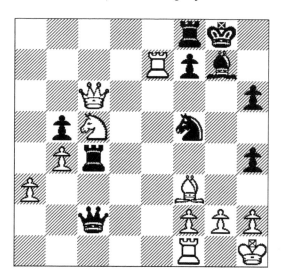

Here Tal played 33. Rxf7?, which should be losing after 33...Rxf7(of course, 33...Kxf7?? 34. Qe6 mates) 34. Bd5 Qe2!(defending the e8-square) 35. Rg1 Qe7 36. Qxb5 Rc2. Many other moves, for example 33. Re8 or 33. Ree1 leave white better. An example of an 'over-tactical' Tal.

Tal-Ragozin, Leningrad 1956

274) Black to play

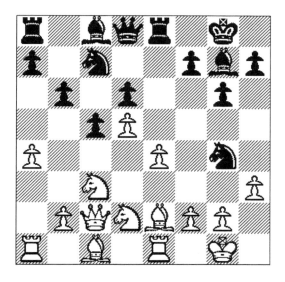

14...Nxf2!, great move, does not leave white much choice:
a) the best defence is 15. Nf3!, but after black captures with the bishop on c3 and then with the knight on e4 he should be slightly better
b) 15. Bxf3 Qh4, followed by Nxh3+, with huge attack
c) 15. Kxf2 Qh4+ 16. Ke1 Bd4! 17. Nd1(only move defending from mate) Qxh3! 18. Bf3 Qh2, followed by f5, and white will not resist much longer

Gurgenidze-Tal, Moscow 1957

275) White to play

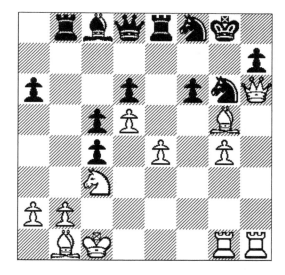

30. e5! is the key move, winning easily in all lines:
a) 30...fxg5 31. Bxg6 hxg6(31...Nxg6 32. Qxh7+ and Qxg6) 32. Qh8+ Kf7 33. Rh7+ Nxh7 34. Qxh7+ Kf8 35. Rf1+ with mate to follow
b) 30...dxe5 31. Bxg6 hxg6 32. Qh8+ Kf7 33. Rh7+! Nxh7 34. Qxh7+ Kf8 35. Bh6#
c) 30...Rxe5 31. Bxg6 Rb7 32. Ne4 and white has too many attacking pieces for

black to hope defending; if black captures on g5 with either piece on the 31st move, 32. Bxh7+ is decisive, while on 31...hxg6 32. Rf1!, threatening 33. Qh8+ with subsequent capture on f6, ends the fight

Tal-Tolush, Moscow 1957

276) Black to play

There are other winning lines too, but what Tal chose is very elegant.
35...Rd8! 36. Bd6 Re8 37. Kh1 Qe2 and now:
a) 38. Rg1 Nf3
b) 38. Rc1 Qe1+ with mate to follow
c) 38. Qf5+ Kg8 39. Qd5+ Kh8 40. Kg1 Rd2! 41. Qxb7 Rd1

Aronson-Tal, Moscow 1957

277) White to play

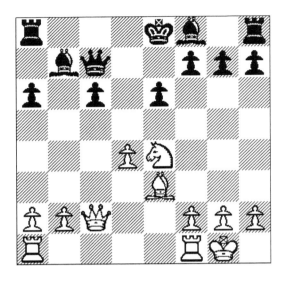

17. d5!, a timely break that does not allow black to consolidate. After 17...exd5(nothing better positionally available) 18. Re1! black can not defend, for example 18...Be7 19. Bc5, and now on 19...Kf8, white has 20. Ng5!

Tal-Milev, Munich 1958

278) Black to play

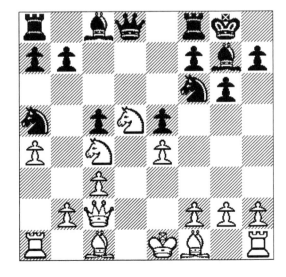

11...Nxe4! 12. Nxa5 Qxd5 13. Bc4 Qd8 14. Qxe4 Qxa5 wins a pawn with some chances to retain it and get an advantage. 12. Qxe4 Bf5 13. Qe2 Nb3! is even worse.

Walther-Tal, Munich 1958

279) White to play

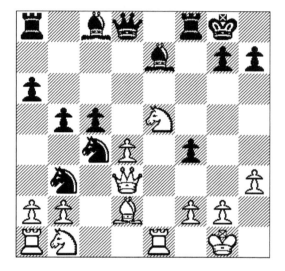

Recapturing with the queen or pawn on b3 could only suit black, who has the bishop pair. Correct is **19. Nc6!** Nxa1 20. Nxd8 Bf5 21. Qf3 Raxd8(Bxd8? Qxa8) 22. Rxe7 Bxb1 23. Bxf4 and, because of the vulnerability of the 2 black minors on the edge on a1 and b1, white has clear advantage.

Tal-Panno, Portoroz 1958

280) White to play

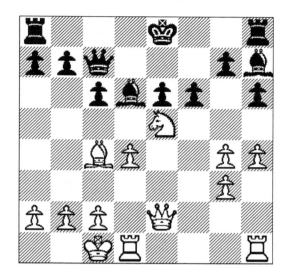

17. Bxe6!! leaves the black king in the center. After 17...fxe5 18. dxe5 Be7 19. g5! white wins, with Qh5+ and Rhf1 both threatening. On 18...Bxe5 19. Rd7!(19. Rhe1 Rd8 is much weaker, as trades will help the defending side) Qa5 20. Rxb7, followed by Re1, is very convincing. On the other hand, if white misses the sacrifice, retreating the knight with 17. Nf3? allows black to castle, which after 17...0-0-0 18. Be6+ Kb8 gives him the upper hand, as he has the pair of bishops, with the g3-pawn loose.

Tal-Fuster, Portoroz 1958

281) White to play

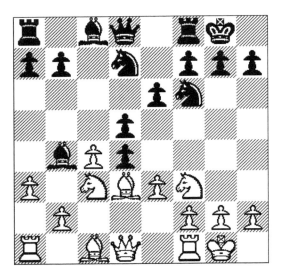

9. Nxd5! is a very unusual tactics, leaving white significantly better after 9...exd5 10. axb4 dxc4 11. Bxc4 Nb6 12. Bb3 dxe3 13. Bxe3. The alternatives are not good. 9. exd4 Bxc3 10. bxc3 dxc4 11. Bxc4 Qc7 is perfectly fine for black, while 9. axb4 dxc3 10. cxd5 cxb2! 11. Bxb2 exd5 is more or less equal too.

Tal-Tolush, Riga 1958

282) White to play

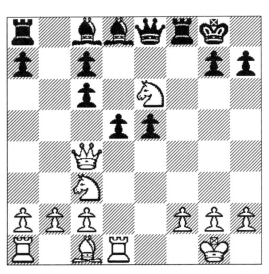

If the queen retreats, recapturing on e6 leaves black with a pawn more plus positional advantage. 16. Nxg7 Kxg7 gives black big positional advantage in the form of the bishop pair and strong center. The only move that leads to more or less equal game is **16. Nxc7!**, although after 16...Bxc7 17. Nxd5 cxd5 18. Qxc7 Rf7 and Bb7 only black could be better due to his superior center, promising attacking chances.

Tal-Furman, Riga 1958

283) Black to play

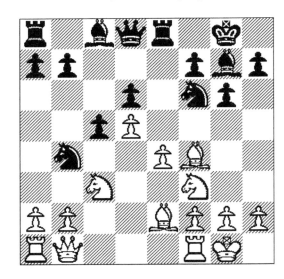

Tal played here the dubious 12...Nxe4?, which after 13. Nxe4 Bf5 14. Nfd2 Nxd5 15. Bg5! leaves black on the verge of a loss(15...Qxg5 16. Nxg5 Bxb1 17. Bc4! and black can not retreat the knight, as Bxf7+ fork decides). Of course, Tal is not Stockfish.

Averbakh-Tal, Riga 1958

166

284) White to play

The simple recapture 16. Rxh1 wins now, but white has much more convincing and much more effective with **16. gxf6!!** and now:
a) 16...Rh7 17. fxg7 Rxg7 18. Nb3
b) 16...Rxd1+ is even weaker, as after 17. Nxd1!(attacking the queen) Qxd2 18. fxg7! white suddenly threatens to promote the g-pawn with check, mating. The best black would have is 18...Be6 19. g8Q+ Kd7 20. Qxc8+ Kxc8 21. Bxd2, and white is left with 2 minor pieces more.

Tal-NN, Stuttgart 1958

285) Black to play

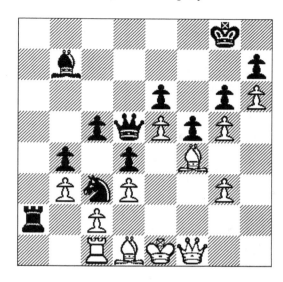

Black has tremendous positional advantage, but this looks like kind of a fortress position. If black does not find a way to break, this might very well end in a draw. Therefore, **45...c4!!**, brilliant. 46. bxc4? Qa5, followed by b3, wins immediately. Black should win also after 46. dxc4 Qa5, although it might take quite some time to do so. The important thing is to understand the breaking method is obligatory.

Mieses-Tal, Soviet Union 1958

286) Black to play

Stockfish gives here alternative lines like 17...Bd7 18. exd5 Bf8 as better tries for black to hold, but Tal played 17...Ng4?, which is losing after 18. fxg4! Qxg5 19. exd5 Bd7 20. Ne4. Even weaker is 19...Bxg4 20. d6! threatening a deadly fork on d7. Accepting the queen sacrifice, on the other hand, is weak, as after 18. Bxd8? Nf2+ 19. Kg1 Nxd1+ 20. Kh1(Kf1 Ne3+ is a royal fork) Nf2+ 21. Kg1 Rexd8 black has at least a slight advantage due to different existing threats, before all a discovered check.

Mititelu-Tal, Varna 1958

287) Black to play

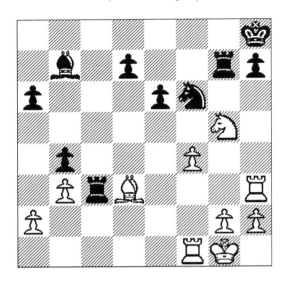

Here Tal continued with 37...e5?!, which Stockfish assesses as fully equal after 38. Rh6 exf4 39. h4 Ng4 40. Rxh7 Rxh7 41. Bxh7. A bunch of other moves, even **37...Kg8**, would have kept black a positional advantage, avoiding exchanges, after all black has more central pawns.

Olafsson-Tal, Bled 1959

288) White to play

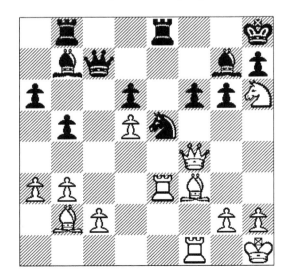

Here Tal played 24. Be4?!, which is losing after 24...g5 25. Qf5 Bxh6 26. Qxf6+ Bg7, black having a piece more. Alternative lines, for example **24. h4**(to stop g6-g5) Qxc2 25. Bxe5! dxe5 26. Nf7+ Kg8 27. Nh6+ Bxh6(27...Kf8? 28. Qb4+ Re7 29. Rxe5!) 28. Qxh6, should give white better chances of salvation.

Tal-Smyslov, Bled 1959

289) Black to play

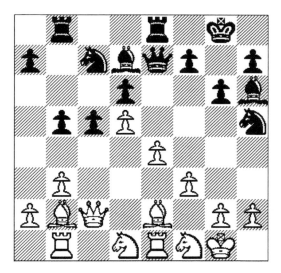

Tal played 18...Nxd5?!, which Stockfish assesses as favouring white after 19. exd5 Bf5 20. Qc3 Bg7 21. Qc1 Bxb1 22. Qxb1, and indeed, white has two minor pieces for the rook and should be able to untangle. An alternative move like **18...Nf4**, followed by a capture on e2, is seemingly a better try to get fully equal.

Gligoric-Tal, Bled 1959

290) Black to play

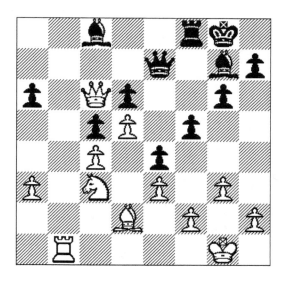

25...f4!! is an astounding and extremely powerful break. The win is there in all lines:
a) 26. exf4 e3! 27. fxe3 Bxc3 28. Bxc3 Qxe3+
b) 26. gxf4 Qh4!, followed by Bh3, and white has weak light-square complex around his king
c) 26. Rb8 fxe3 27. Bxe3 Bh3 28. Rxf8+ Qxf8, and white is helpless due to the double threat of Qf3 and Bxc3

Benko-Tal, Bled 1959

291) White to play

19. Qxf7!! is the key move:
a) 19...Rxf7?? 20. Rxd8+ mates
b) 19...Qa1+ 20. Kd2 Rxf7 21. Nxf7+
Kg8 22. Rxa1 Kxf7 23. Ne5+ leaves
white the exchange up
Alternatives don't win, for example 19.
Rxd8?? Qa1+ 20. Kd2 Rxd8+, or 19.
Nxf7+? Kg8, though the latter line is a
bit mind-boggling.

Tal-Smyslov, Bled 1959

292) White to play

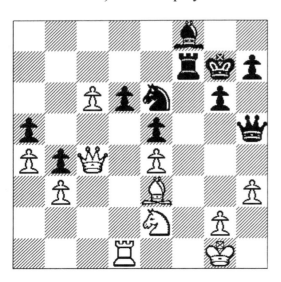

Here Tal blundered with 32. Qxe6?,
which leads only to a perpetual after
32...Qxe2 33. Bh6+ Kh8 34. Qxf7
Qxd1+ 35. Kf2 Bxh6 36. c7 Qd2+ 37.
Kf1 Qd1+. Winning is **32. Rf1!**, very
subtle move, 32...Rxf1+ 33. Kxf1 Nc7
34. Bb6

Tal-Dauga, Riga 1959

293) White to play

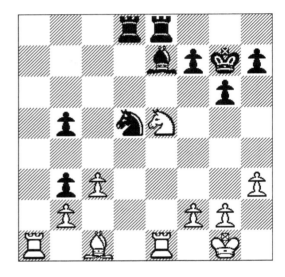

28. Bh6+! wins by force in all lines:
a) 28...Kxh6 29. Nxf7+ Kg7 30. Nxd8
Rxd8 31. Ra5 Rb8 32. Ra7! Kf6 33.
Rd7. In above line, 32. Re5? instead is
a mistake, as black has the surprising
32...Bd8, counter-attacking the a5-
rook, 33. Ra7 Nc7 with most probable
draw.
b) 28...Kf6?? 29. Ng4+ Kf5 30. Re5#
c) 28...Kg8 29. Nc6 Rc8 30. Rd1 Rxc6
31. Rxd5 Rc7 32. Rxb5 with clear
outcome

Tal-Bronstein, Tbilisi 1959

170

294) Black to play

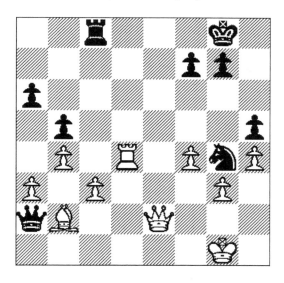

Tal played 36...Rxc3?!, which Stockfish says is a straightforward draw after 37. Rd8+ Kh7 38. Qe4+ g6 39. Qc2!(very elegant, only engine can see that) Rxg3+(Rxc2?? Rh8#) 40. Kh1 Rh3+ with a perpetual. **36...Nf6**, intending Re8, not forcing things, promised black better chances to get the full point in a longer struggle.

Vasiukov-Tal, Tbilisi 1959

295) Black to play

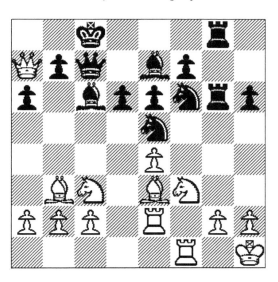

Here Tal played 21...Nxe4?, which Stockfish sees as winning for white after 22. Nxe4 Bxe4 23. Bb6! Nc6 24. Qa8+ Kd7 25. Qxg8 Rxg8 26. Bxc7 Bxf3 27. Rxf3 Nd4 28. Bb6. If black deviates in above line with 23...Qc6?, then 24. Rxe4! Qxe4 25. Qa8+ Kd7 26. Ba4+! Qxa4 27. Qxb7+ mates in a couple of moves.

Nikitin-Tal, Tbilisi 1959

296) White to play

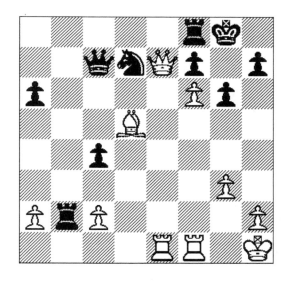

25. Re6! decides:
a) 25...fxe6?? 26. Qg7#
b) 25...Qd8 26. Rd6
c) 25...Rb7 26. Rd6 Ra7 27. Rf4!, threatening Rxc4 and black has no defence, 27...Nc5 28. Bxf7+ Rxf7 29. Rd8+

Tal-Darga, Hamburg 1960

297) White to play

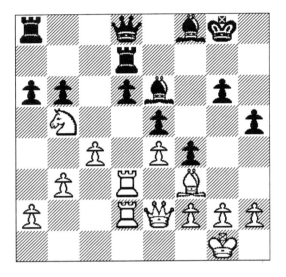

Retreating with the knight to c3 will hardly give even the slightest winning chances, so attempting a trap with **24. Nxd6!?** is well worth it. Now, 24...Bxd6? 25. Qd1! Raa7 26. Rxd6 wins a pawn. 24...Qc7! 25. Qd1 Qc6, however, is fully equal.

Tal-Ghitescu, Leipzig 1960

298) White to play

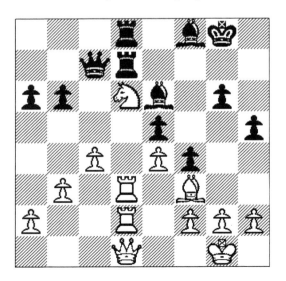

As if the knight is lost, but **26. Ne8!** Rxd3 27. Nxc7 Rxd2 28. Qa1 Bf7 29. Nd5 saves it, leading to fully equal with a bit more depth after 29...Bxd5 30. exd5 Bc5 31. Qxe5 Rxf2 32. Qe6+ Kg7 33. Qe5+ Kg8 34. Qe6+ with a perpetual.

Tal-Ghitescu, Leipzig 1960

299) White to play

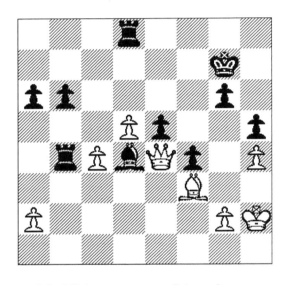

36. d6! is very powerful, and now:
a) 36...Rxd6 37. Qb7+ Kf8 38. Bd5; if 37...Kh6?, then 38. Qc8, threatening mate on h8
b) 36...Kh6 37. Qd5 Rb1 38. Qf7! Bg1+ 39. Kh3 Bf2 40. g3
In both cases, white should be winning.

Tal-Ghitescu, Leipzig 1960

300) White to play

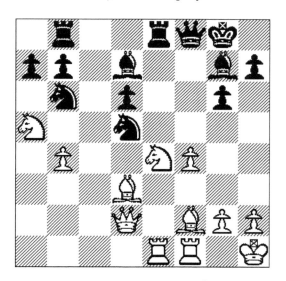

Tal played here 26. Bc4!?, which wins at least a pawn after 26...Nxc4?! 27. Nxc4 Nf6 28. Ned6 Rxe1 29. Rxe1. In above line, however, black can continue better with 26...Be6! and in the unimaginable complications it is unclear if white is on top or not. Therefore, the best move above is **26. Nc4!**, and after 26...Bf5(seemingly nothing better) 27. Bxb6 Nxb6 28. Ncxd6 white is clearly winning.

Tal-Contendini, Leipzig 1960

www.ingramcontent.com/pod-product-compliance
Lightning Source LLC
LaVergne TN
LVHW080116070326
832902LV00015B/2628